The Beauty and Glory
of the Father

The Beauty and Glory
of the Father

Edited by
Joel R. Beeke

Reformation Heritage Books
Grand Rapids, Michigan

Published by
Reformation Heritage Books
2965 Leonard St. NE
Grand Rapids, MI 49525
616-977-0889 / Fax 616-285-3246
e-mail: orders@heritagebooks.org
website: www.heritagebooks.org

ISBN: 978-1-60178-246-5

Printed in the United States of America
13 14 15 16 17 18/10 9 8 7 6 5 4 3 2 1

Library of Congress Control Number: 2013941406

For additional Reformed literature, request a free book list
from Reformation Heritage Books at the above address.

With heartfelt appreciation for

Rev. Maarten Kuivenhoven

former student, loyal friend, and faithful colleague.
You are a joy to know and co-labor with;
I pray God that we may work together
for many more years on behalf of our Savior's bride.

—JRB

Contents

Preface

Christ came to give sinners access to the Father (Eph. 2:18). God sent His Son to redeem them for adoption as God's children, and He sent His Spirit to make that adoption a heartfelt reality (Gal. 4:4–6). Therefore, when the Lord Jesus taught His disciples to pray, His first words were, "Our Father" (Matt. 6:9). The fatherhood of God is a consolation of infinite sweetness to the believer.

Knowing God as our Father by adoption highlights the vast privileges of every Christian. William Perkins (1558–1602) said that a believer should esteem his adoption as God's child to be greater than being the child or heir of any earthly king, since the son of the greatest emperor may be under God's wrath, but the child of God has Christ as his older brother, the Holy Spirit as his comforter, and the kingdom of heaven as his inheritance. Yet few people realize this experientially. Perkins said: "At earthly preferments men will stand amazed; but seldom shall you find a man that is ravished with joy in this, that he is the child of God. But…we must learn to have more joy in being the sons of God, than to be heirs of any worldly kingdom."[1]

We had the privilege of rejoicing in the Father at the August 2012 conference of Puritan Reformed Theological Seminary. Nearly five hundred people sat at the feet of Jesus Christ and listened as He revealed His Father. We thank God for working through the preaching of the Scriptures by the faculty, visiting professors, and friends

---

1. William Perkins, *A Clovvd of Faithfvll VVitnesses, Leading to the Heauenly Canaan: Or, A Commentarie upon the 11. Chapter to the Hebrewes*, in *The Workes of that Famovs and VVorthy Minister of Christ in the Vniuersitie of Cambridge, Mr. William Perkins*, 3 vols. (London: Iohn Legatt and Cantrell Ligge, 1612–13), 3:138 (2nd set of pagination).

of the seminary. Each of the chapters in this book represents a message presented at that conference.[2]

We saw the beauty of the Father shining in His beloved Son, Jesus Christ. Rev. Bartel Elshout led us to exult over many biblical testimonies that all things, from creation to redemption to final glorification, revolve around the Father's love for His Son. Dr. Jerry Bilkes traced the vivid image of God calling "my son out of Egypt" (Hos. 11:1) from the life of ancient Israel to the life of Christ and to our lives today.

We adored the Father for His glory. Dr. Derek Thomas pressed upon our hearts the fear of the Lord and the knowledge of the Holy One as revealed in Isaiah's vision (Isa. 6). Dr. William Van Doodewaard preached an exposition of the Father's merciful gift of regeneration unto an indestructible inheritance (1 Peter 1:3–5). Rev. Paul Smalley refreshed our souls from the wells of Richard Sibbes's teaching on the mercy and faithfulness of the Father.

We grew in our knowledge of the Father as our Savior God. Dr. Thomas led us in a rich theological meditation on seeing the Father in the face of Jesus. I presented our adoption by God and opened up several practical applications from it with the assistance of the Puritans.

We found rest in the guiding and providing hands of our Father in heaven. Dr. VanDoodewaard taught on our heavenly Father in the Sermon on the Mount. Dr. David Murray drew out some implications of God's fatherhood for biblical counseling. Rev. Burk Parsons showed us the beauty of tough love in the Father's discipline of His children.

We also wrapped up the Trinitarian theme of the last three conferences on the beauty and glory of the Father, the Son, and the Holy Spirit.[3] Rev. Ryan McGraw challenged us to shape all our piety—the old and precious word for godliness of heart and life—with the tri-personal character of our God. He also challenged us to examine ourselves so as to discern whether we as individuals are saved by this God through the only Mediator.

---

2. Many of the audio recordings of these talks may be found at www.sermonaudio.com by searching under "PRTS conference 2012."

3. See *The Beauty and Glory of Christ*, ed. Joel R. Beeke (Grand Rapids: Reformation Heritage Books, 2011); and *The Beauty and Glory of the Holy Spirit*, ed. Joel R. Beeke and Joseph A. Pipa Jr. (Grand Rapids: Reformation Heritage Books, 2012).

The fatherhood of God is inextricably intertwined with the gospel of our Lord Jesus Christ. Perkins said that the purpose of the gospel is to reveal God "not only as a Creator, but as a Father," and to draw us to know Him as "our Father in Christ; and consequently to carry ourselves as dutiful children to him in all subjection and obedience. They which do not this, know not the intent of the gospel."[4]

We are delighted now to offer you the substance of these messages in printed form. Many thanks go to Greg Bailey for his assistance in editing, Gary den Hollander for proofing, Lois Haley for transcribing several addresses, Linda den Hollander and Kim DeMeester for typesetting, and Amy Zevenbergen for the cover design.

If you can, consider joining us at future PRTS conferences.[5] Please also pray for the work of the seminary, that God's Spirit would fill the faculty, staff, and students with love, faithfulness to the Scriptures, holiness of life, and power for ministry.

May God use these addresses to draw you in the Spirit through Christ to the Father, that you may delight in His sovereign love and respond with childlike love and obedience.

—Joel R. Beeke

---

4. Perkins, *A Commentarie or Exposition vpon the Five First Chapters of the Epistle to the Galatians*, in *Workes*, 2:164.

5. See www.puritanseminary.org for more information.

SEEING THE
FATHER'S GLORY
IN HIS ONLY
BEGOTTEN SON

CHAPTER 1

The Father's Love for His Son

Bartel Elshout

The Father loveth the Son.
—John 3:35

The third chapter of John's gospel records Jesus' discourse with Nicodemus about the necessity of the new birth (vv. 1–13), His articulation of the biblical gospel (vv. 14–21), and John the Baptist's profound testimony about Christ (vv. 22–36)—words that marked the conclusion of John the Baptist's public ministry. In this final segment of the chapter, amid John the Baptist's moving confession that Christ must increase and he decrease (v. 30) and the solemn declaration that God's wrath abides on all who do not believe the Son (v. 36), we find these profound words: "The Father loveth the Son" (v. 35). This statement stands out for its beautiful simplicity, but the truth it contains is so extraordinary that it excels everything else in this chapter—even the fact that God so loved the world that He gave His only begotten Son. These words tell us why God the Father was moved to give His Son to be the Savior of a fallen world: because He loves His Son!

The Father's Love for His Son: The Fountain of All Theology
The Holy Spirit gives us a glimpse into the infinite depth of the Father's heart—a heart that is eternally moved in love for His eternally begotten and beloved Son. This is the fountain from which all theology flows. Nothing so precisely defines who the Father is as the fact that He loves His Son with the totality and fullness of His divine person.

No book in the New Testament highlights this love relationship between the Father and the Son so much as the gospel of John. There are at least 126 direct and indirect references to the Father/

Son relationship, and this gospel states eight times explicitly that the Father loves His Son (John 3:35; 5:20; 10:17; 15:9, 10; 17:23, 24, 26).

The remainder of the New Testament repeatedly focuses on this essential and foundational truth regarding the identity and character of the Father, as, for instance in Romans 15:6: "That ye may with one mind and one mouth glorify God, even the Father of our Lord Jesus Christ" (cf. 2 Cor. 1:3; 11:31; Eph. 1:3; 3:14; Col. 1:3; 1 Peter 1:3; 2 John 3). Given that we observe throughout Scripture that God does what He does because He is who He is (e.g., Pss. 25:8; 86:5; 119:68), and in light of the above testimony, it follows that this is supremely and profoundly applicable to the fact that the Father loves the Son. In other words, the Father's eternal decrees are directly related to the fact that He loves His Son. From eternity, the Father of our Lord Jesus Christ delighted Himself in the Son of His good pleasure, who is "the brightness of his glory, and the express image of his person" (Heb. 1:3). In Proverbs 8:30, Christ says, "I was daily his [the Father's] delight, rejoicing always before him."

Paul tells us in Colossians 1:18–19 that it has been the Father's eternal delight that His Son should have the preeminence, and that "it pleased the Father that in him should all fulness dwell." This preeminence of the Son should not be construed to mean that the glory of the Father and the Holy Spirit are less than the glory of the Son; rather, in the Son we behold the supreme and most magnificent display of His Father's glory. That is why the Father so delights in His Son and has "given him a name which is above every name" (Phil. 2:9). Jesus expressed this in His High Priestly Prayer: "I have glorified thee on the earth.... And now, O Father, glorify thou me with thine own self with the glory which I had with thee before the world was" (John 17:4–5).

In other words, the Father is eternally engaged in glorifying His Son so that His Son will ever be the fullest and most superlative expression of who He is as the Father. The Father is well pleased with His Son because the Son is a perfect reflection of Himself. As He beholds His Son, the Father knows Himself perfectly.

The Son: The Eternal, Infinite Object of the Father's Love
In light of this special relationship between the Father and the Son, we conclude that the Trinity is a love relationship. The Father, in the

person of the Holy Spirit, communicates the full essence of His love and person to the Son, and the Son, also in the person of the Holy Spirit, reciprocates and communicates the full essence of His love and person to the Father.

The Spirit, therefore, is the bond of love that unites the Father and the Son in this everlasting relationship. This explains why the Scriptures testify that the Spirit proceeds from both the Father and the Son, for there is unbroken fellowship between the two. As the Spirit proceeds from the Father, the Father communicates His love to the Son; and as the Spirit proceeds from the Son, the Son communicates His love to the Father. The Father and the Son know and love each other in a full, comprehensive sense through the Spirit.

On several occasions, Christ explicitly referred to this love relationship between Himself and His Father: "No man knoweth the Son, but the Father; neither knoweth any man the Father, save the Son" (Matt. 11:27); "No man knoweth who the Son is, but the Father; and who the Father is, but the Son" (Luke 10:22); "As the Father knoweth me, even so know I the Father" (John 10:15). In this eternal relationship, the Father and the Son, in the Spirit, experience eternal and complete satisfaction in each other.

We need to understand, however, that the Scriptures highlight the Father's love for His Son in that relationship. Twice during Christ's sojourn on earth, the Father testified from heaven with an audible voice: "This is my beloved Son, in whom I am well pleased" (Matt. 3:17; 17:5). The focus is especially on the Father loving and glorifying the Son, beholding in Him the brilliant and comprehensive display of the glory and magnificence of His own person.

How appropriate it is that the Son should be the object of His Father's love. The Father, whose personality and attributes are of infinite dimension, must have a suitable object for His eternal and infinite love. He finds it in His Son, who is fully coequal with Him in the infinity and magnificence of all His attributes, and whom He, in the Spirit, therefore loves with all the infinite love of His divine person.

The Father's Love for His Son: The Preeminent Motive for All His Divine Activity

Since God does what He does because He is who He is, it follows that the Father's infinite love for the Son of His bosom (John 1:18) is the motive for all that He does. This love governs all His activity from eternity past until eternity future; it motivates Him to glorify His Son in all that He undertakes.

We need to apply this first of all to the work of creation, for it was love for His Son that moved the Father to create the universe for His Son. Paul writes in Colossians 1:16 that all things were created not only by the Son, but also that all things were created *for* Him. The entire universe, with all of its visible and invisible realities, was created for the Son—it all was an expression of the Father's infinite love for His Son. It was His gift of love. Therefore, upon finishing the work of creation, the Father saw that it was "very good" (Gen. 1:31).

Creation: A Reflection of the Glory of God's Son

What made the work of creation so "very good" in the eyes of the Father? The answer is that He saw the glory of His beloved Son reflected in all He had made. That all of creation reflected the glory of His Son is confirmed by the fact that the Father spoke the universe into existence. This means that all creation is an expression of His Word. In each star and each insect, the wisdom of God is on display.

The Son is also the eternal Word of the Father, and was in the beginning; therefore, the words by which God spoke everything into existence were ultimately a reflection of the Living Word, the Father's well-beloved Son. How beautifully this truth is expressed in Psalm 19:1–3: "The heavens declare the glory of God; and the firmament sheweth his handiwork. Day unto day uttereth speech, and night unto night sheweth knowledge. There is no speech nor language, where their voice is not heard." This means that all of creation is the Father's speech to us—a speech that communicates His Word to us every day and night.

Thus, the Father's only begotten Son is the focal point of all God's eternal purposes. All things must work together to the accomplishment of the singular and overarching goal of all that the Father has sovereignly purposed. There is therefore nothing arbitrary about the exercise of His sovereignty, for in exercising it He is always aiming for the glory of the Son whom He loves. To accomplish that is the purpose of the Father's sovereign good pleasure.

Adam: The Created Son of God, Bearing the Image
of the Eternal Son of God

This is also evident when we consider the creation of man, the masterpiece of God's creative work. The Father's love for His Son, the love that moved Him to create the entire universe *for* His Son, also moved Him to create Adam in the image of His Son.

We arrive at this conclusion by comparing Scripture with Scripture. In Romans 8:29, Paul tells us that the reason why all things must work together for good (v. 28) is to be found in the fact that those whom the Father had foreknown, "he also did predestinate to be conformed to the image of his Son." In other words, the ultimate goal of redemption is the conformity of fallen human beings to the image of the Father's well-beloved Son. This is confirmed in 1 John 3:2, where John writes, "Beloved, now are we the sons of God, and it doth not yet appear what we shall be: but we know that, when he shall appear, we shall be like him; for we shall see him as he is." Consequently, those who have been predestined to be conformed to the image of God's Son will one day be like Him.

If the goal of the Father's redemptive work is to conform men and women to the image of His Son, this must have been His original goal in creating man. In Revelation 4:11, it is stated explicitly that "thou hast created all things, and for thy pleasure they are and were created." We know that it is the Father's pleasure to glorify the Son of His love. This text tells us, however, that all that God does now and has done in the past has one common goal; the goals of creation and redemption are the same. When we listen to the divine dialogue in Genesis 1:26, we are listening to a conversation between the Father and the Son (in the Spirit): "Let us make man in our image, after our likeness." Romans 8:29 specifically instructs us, however, that this must mean that Adam was made in the image of God's Son. This does not at all contradict the language of Genesis 1:26, for in bearing the image of God's Son, Adam also reflected the image of the Father. We can conclude this from the words of Christ, when He stated that whoever has seen Him has seen the Father (John 14:9).

This explains why Scripture also refers to Adam as the son of God (Luke 3:38), for in him the Father beheld a perfect reflection of the glory of His Son; Adam, as the created son of God, bore the image of the natural Son of God. This is what made him the masterpiece of

God's creation. Though all of creation reflected the Son's glory, Adam did so in a way far superior to everything else God had made. That is why man was the crowning piece of the Father's creative activity.

If the entire universe was created *for* the Father's Son, then this was true for Adam in a far more profound way! Adam was expressly created by the Father not only to reflect Christ's glory, but also to delight in Him, the Living Word (John 1:1). The Father created him with the intellectual and spiritual faculties to know, love, and serve the Son, and this made Adam uniquely different from the rest of creation.

This is what constituted the bliss of Adam and Eve, for it was in the person of His Son that the Father revealed Himself to them and communicated with them. John 1:18 tells us that "no man hath seen God at any time; the only begotten Son, which is in the bosom of the Father, he hath declared him." If no man has ever seen God in His spiritual essence, then this includes Adam and Eve. Therefore, the only begotten Son of God, being eternally in the heart of His Father, declared the Father to Adam and Eve. It was in the person of His Son that the Father entered into a father-child relationship with Adam and Eve, and daily communed with them.

We may therefore conclude that, before the fall, Adam and Eve delighted themselves in the very same Son of God in whom the Father eternally delights Himself. Being the bearers of the image of His Son, loving and worshiping Him, Adam and Eve were the recipients of the love the Father has for His Son. The Father beheld the reflection of His eternal Son and loved them with the same love with which He loved His Son, for in John 14:21, Jesus tells us that "he that loveth me shall be loved of my Father." If this is true for redeemed sinners who love the Son with an imperfect love, how much more this must have been true for Adam and Eve, who loved God's Son perfectly.

In summary, the Father created man for His Son and in His image in order that man might know and love His Son and live for His glory. That truly pleases the Father, who loves His Son, which explains why His delights are in the children of men (Prov. 8:31).

The Wretchedness of Man's Fall: The Loss of the Image of God's Son

How well Satan understood that God the Father was supremely glorified by man as the bearer of the image of His Son! If John Bunyan

is correct in his spiritual allegory in *The Holy War*, then Satan was
the chief angel who aspired after the glory of God's Son. That rebellion prompted the Father to expel Satan, as well as the angels that
supported his rebellion, permanently from His presence. The Father
could not tolerate in His presence a creature that challenged the
glory and preeminence of His beloved Son.

From that moment forward, Satan became the sworn enemy of
God's Son, and all of history has become the battleground on which
Satan has waged war against Him (Gen. 3:15). It should therefore
come as no surprise that he immediately took aim at the one creature who bore the image of God's Son. He sought to take vengeance
for having been expelled from God's presence by taking direct aim
at the heart of God. He knew that in causing man to fall, he would
rob the Father of the joy of having man resemble His Son and live
for His glory.

This is what makes the fall of man so wretched. How supremely
offensive man became to the Father once he lost the image of His Son
and no longer lived for His glory! How man's unbelief and rebellion, both now and then, provokes the Father to wrath—a Father who
loves His Son! How righteous the Father would therefore have been
if He had irreversibly rejected and damned a fallen humanity that
rejects His Son in unbelief. And yet, it pleased Him not to do so. This
is all the more remarkable when we consider that this is precisely
what the Father has done with Satan and his fallen angels. For them,
there is no redemption; their eternal perdition is forever sealed.

Why does the Father deal so kindly with the children of men?
Why did He purpose to redeem fallen mankind rather than fallen
angels? The answer is to be found in the fact that the Father loves
His Son. The striking difference between angels and men is that the
angels were not created in the image of God's beloved Son. Man,
however, was—and so God redeems fallen human beings who have
lost that image to transform them once again to the image of His
Son, Jesus Christ. Because He loves His Son, He eternally purposed
to vindicate the honor of the Son by redeeming fallen human beings
to become again what He created them to be: bearers of the image of
His Son who know, love, serve, and glorify Him. This confirms there
is nothing arbitrary about God's eternal decrees and purposes, for

the great objective of His sovereign purpose in redeeming the children of men is the glory of the Son He loves.

The Father Giving the Son of His Eternal Love
for the Redemption of Fallen Sinners

If the profundity of all this overwhelms us, how can we begin to comprehend the work of redemption? How can it be that the Father, who loves His Son with a love that transcends our comprehension, would send this Son into the world to redeem fallen sons and daughters of Adam? How can we comprehend that the Father chose *fallen* men (Eph. 1:4) to become the recipients of the love He has for His Son (John 17:26) and to be conformed to His image (Rom. 8:29), knowing that the very object of His love would have to become the object of His infinite wrath in order to redeem them? Yet the eternal Son of God became the Son of Man for that very purpose.

What a wonder it was when the Holy Spirit, who proceeds from the Father and the Son, overshadowed Mary and caused the miraculous conception of the Christ! The angel Gabriel testified of this to an astonished Mary, saying, "The Holy Ghost shall come upon thee, and the power of the Highest shall overshadow thee: therefore also that holy thing which shall be born of thee shall be called the Son of God" (Luke 1:35). The moment this came to pass, the second Adam was fashioned within her and the eternal Son of God became the created Son of God (as was Adam) in the one person of Immanuel—God with us.

At that blessed moment, a moment on which the entire history of mankind pivots, God and man were united in the person of Christ with a bond that cannot and will not be severed for all eternity. What an extraordinary reality it is that the eternal Word of the Father was made flesh—that the beloved Son of the Father took upon Himself our humanity. The eternal Son of God became the Son of man in order that sons and daughters of men might become sons and daughters of the living God, bearing the image of the Son of God. In short, the Son of God became like us, in order that we might become like Him. Great is the mystery of godliness: God was manifest in the flesh (1 Tim. 3:16).

To accomplish all this, and to see to it that His Father's good pleasure would prosper, the Son had to be nailed to the cross and there descend into the depths of hell, crying out from this awful abyss,

"My God, my God, why hast *thou* [My Father] forsaken *me* [Thy Son]?" (Matt. 27:46). How unspeakable must that suffering have been for Him who had eternally been in His Father's bosom, but what must it have been for the Father when He had to hide His face from His beloved Son? Yet for the sake of all who have been chosen by the Father in Him, it had to be so. Only by the Father's beloved Son experiencing the essence of hell could the groundwork be laid for the adoption of fallen sinners.

What joy there was in the Father's heart when He perceived that His Son had finished the work He had given Him to do! When Christ uttered these precious words, "It is finished," and then commended His spirit into His Father's hands, the Father could not restrain Himself any longer, and with His mighty hands He rent the veil of separation in the temple (Matt. 27:51), declaring His full approval of the sacrifice of the Son of His love. On the basis of that finished work, the Father could forever remove the wall of separation between Himself and the children of men.

These are matters that cause our minds to reel. How can we begin to grasp that the Father eternally gave redeemed rebels to the Son in order that through them the glory of His Son would shine forth most brilliantly? In order to accomplish this, He made His beloved Son, who knew no sin, become sin for us, so that vile sinners, so utterly unworthy of such a favor, might be made the righteousness of God in Him (2 Cor. 5:21), and become the adopted sons and daughters of God. What an astonishing truth: the Son of God, who as the second Adam is also the Son of Man, will forever be the Elder Brother of the Father's adopted children. In Him they will forever belong to His Father's family.

Here words fail, and we must cry out in holy amazement with the apostle Paul, "O the depth of the riches both of the wisdom and knowledge of God! how unsearchable are his judgments, and his ways past finding out! For who hath known the mind of the Lord? or who hath been his counsellor?" (Rom. 11:33–34).

The Goal of the Father's Plan of Redemption:
The Glory of His Son

In the midst of our failure to grasp these mysteries, one truth emerges: the entire plan and work of redemption revolves around the Father's

Son, the Lord Jesus Christ. The gospel is the Father's good news to a fallen world, and by way of the gospel, the Father unveils His precious Son to lost, guilty, and hell-worthy sinners. In the gospel, the Father declares that in His Son He has provided a perfect and complete Mediator through whom fallen sinners can be reconciled with Him, inviting sinners to believe in His Son for the salvation of their souls.

Therefore, the Father's Son, the Lord Jesus Christ, is the sum and substance of the gospel—a gospel in which the Father freely offers His Son to sinners without money and price (Isa. 55:1–2). In this gospel, the Father declares to sinners even today, "This is my beloved Son, in whom I am well pleased; hear ye him" (Matt. 17:5).

Faith in God's Son, the Lord Jesus Christ:
The Unmistakable Fruit of the Spirit's Work
The Father's heart stirs when sinners believe in His Son and put their trust in Him alone for salvation. What joy fills the depth of His being when sinners delight in what He delights in: His Son and His finished work on the cross!

This explains why the Father promises to bestow such extraordinary blessings upon all who believe in His Son. His unconditional promise to them is eternal life (John 3:16). This gift of eternal life encompasses the extraordinary blessings of the full pardon of sin, full reconciliation with the Father, adoption into His family, the abiding presence of His Spirit, and the prospect of dwelling forever in His presence. All this God the Father bestows on sinners who truly believe in His beloved Son, no matter how weak and feeble their faith might be.

It is the hallmark of the saving ministry of His Spirit to work in the heart of sinners in such a fashion that the Father's beloved Son, the Lord Jesus Christ, becomes so irresistibly attractive to them that they confess, "Give me this Jesus, or else I die!" To accomplish this, the Holy Spirit teaches sinners how guilty and lost they are before God, thereby making room in their hearts for the Father's beloved Son. As a fruit of that instruction, sinners see that Jesus Christ is the only solution for guilty and polluted souls. As the Spirit of the Father and the Son, He does not rest until sinners, brought to the end of themselves, embrace Jesus by faith; it is His special work to glorify the Son whom the Father loves (John 16:14–15).

Christ Himself put it this way: "Every man therefore that hath heard, and hath learned of the Father, cometh unto me" (John 6:45). Since the Father loves the Son, it follows that when sinners hear and learn from Him by the Spirit, they come to His Son. Coming to and believing on the Son, the Lord Jesus Christ, is therefore the ultimate proof that the Father, by His Spirit, is accomplishing His saving work in the heart of a sinner.

Faithful Gospel Ministry: The Preaching of Christ, the Father's Beloved Son

Since it is the Father's good pleasure that sinners come to and become like His Son, the focus of the ministry of the Word must be the Son. The great purpose of faithful gospel ministry is always to preach Christ: to invite sinners to come to and close with Him, and to urge believers to abide in Him and follow Him. As the entire solar system revolves around the sun, so every aspect of gospel ministry must revolve around the Father's Son, the blessed Sun of Righteousness. The expression "Christ-centered preaching" in one sense is a redundancy, for preaching that is not truly Son-centered is not true preaching. Preaching that pleases the Father, honors the Son, and is according to the mind of the Spirit always engages in the faithful exegesis of the written Word and always leads us to the Son, the Living Word and the Christ of the Scriptures.

The Father therefore raises up men who bear witness to His Son, so that His Son may be supremely glorified in the hearts and lives of sinners through their ministry. Only when preaching is Christ-centered is the Father glorified, for He is exalted only when His Son is exalted to the highest. The mark of a true minister of the Word is that he is preoccupied with Christ, the Father's Son, with an all-consuming desire to preach this Christ and His unsearchable riches. Such a ministry is endorsed by the Father through His Spirit; such was the ministry of the apostles, of whom we read, "They ceased not to teach and preach Jesus Christ" (Acts 5:42).

The Father chooses to use this kind of faithful, Christ-centered ministry to form a people for Himself, so that Christ, His Son, might be supremely glorified and might be formed within them—all because the Father loves the Son. This and this alone is why He chose His people in His Son, gave them to Him in the eternal counsel of peace, redeems them in Him, unites them to Him, conforms them to Him, and molds them into a people who will eternally delight themselves in Him—a people who will forever worship the Son, "saying with a loud voice, Worthy is the Lamb that was slain to receive power, and riches, and wisdom, and strength, and honour, and glory, and blessing" (Rev. 5:12).

The Son of God, our blessed Lord and Savior Jesus Christ, is the great focal point of God's redemptive purpose toward us. The Father loves us with an eternal love because we are eternally comprehended in His Son. He is *the* Elect in whom the Father delights Himself (Isa. 42:1), and therefore He delights Himself in us, a people chosen in Him. We are the recipients of the love wherewith the Father loves His Son.

The Father loves us because He loves His Son, for He always beholds us in His Son. This is what Paul has in mind when he writes that we are "accepted in the beloved" (Eph. 1:6). This explains the stupendous truth expressed by Christ in His High Priestly Prayer, namely, that the Father loves us with the same love with which He loves His Son (John 17:23, 26). What an extraordinary comfort and privilege this is, for this love is infinite, unchanging, and unwavering! Herein lies the security of God's saints, for nothing shall ever be able to separate them from the love of God that is in Christ Jesus (Rom. 8:35–39).

The Holy Obligation of the Redeemed:
To Love the Father's Son

How can we ever magnify the Father sufficiently for the fact that He was eternally moved within Himself to make us, wretched sinners, the recipients of the love with which He loves His Son—and that, to make this a reality, He gave the Son of His love to be a sacrifice for our sins?

Is this magnificent God not worthy of our love? Should not every fiber of our beings love the Son of God whom the Father loves? Is this not the great purpose for which the Father redeemed us, namely, that we would love and honor His precious Son both now and forever? Should such amazing love not kindle in us a flame of devoted love in return?

Nothing delights and pleases the Father more than when His people love His Son and endeavor to be like Him by His grace. That is the Father's ultimate objective in sanctifying His people: His eternal purpose is that those He has chosen in His Son also bear the image of His Son (Rom. 8:28–29). It is therefore the special work of the Holy Spirit to sanctify the people of God—to conform them to the image of the Father's beloved Son. It is His special work to glorify Christ, the Father's Son, and He is ceaselessly at work in the people of God to bring forth conformity to Him.

This explains why sin so grieves the Spirit of Christ, for when we sin we manifest the very opposite of the image of Christ—something abhorrent to the Father. Whenever we sin, we transgress the written Word of God, and whenever we dishonor the written Word of God, we dishonor the Living Word of God, the Father's well-beloved Son. This is what makes sin so ugly and obnoxious in God's sight. There is nothing more grievous to God than when we dishonor His Son. This is especially true when His people are guilty of this, those He has formed for Himself that they would show forth the glory of His precious Son.

How ruthlessly we ought to deal with sin in our lives, and by God's grace pluck out the eyes and cut off the hands that bring dishonor to His Son! How love for God's Son ought to motivate us to honor Him by keeping His commandments! The Father is filled with unspeakable joy when He beholds in His people the likeness of His well-beloved Son. What a sacred duty of love we have to abide in the Son who gave Himself for us, so that we, as we abide in Him, may bring forth much Christlike fruit to the glory of the Father (John 15:5, 8)!

The Distinguishing Mark of the Adopted Sons and Daughters of God: Love for the Eternal Son of God

In light of these truths, how evident it should be that Christians, as members of the Father's spiritual family, are people who love whom their Father loves—the Son, the Lord Jesus Christ—because the love of God the Father has been shed abroad in their hearts (Rom. 5:5). This is significant, for we have observed that the object of the Father's love is His only begotten Son. This love for His Son truly defines the Father's love, and when He sheds His love in a sinner's heart, and when this love begins to function in the heart of that regenerated sinner, it too has the Son of God as its object.

True believers therefore are always people who love the same Son the Father loves. They are redeemed sinners who are indwelt by the Spirit of the Father and the Son—a Spirit whose special work it is to glorify the Son and show Him to His people (John 16:13–15). This spiritual delight in the Son is the essential ingredient of the communion between the Father and His children, for "can two walk together, except they be agreed?" (Amos 3:3).

As they increasingly and experientially become acquainted with their own wretchedness, true believers become increasingly pre-occupied with the Son of God and His inexpressible beauty; Jesus Christ becomes their all and in all. They love the Son the Father loves and cry out in holy ecstasy: "My beloved is white and ruddy, the chiefest among ten thousand.… His mouth is most sweet: yea, he is altogether lovely. This is my beloved, and this is my friend, O daugh-ters of Jerusalem" (Song 5:10–16). Yes, indeed, they love the Lord Jesus Christ in sincerity (Eph. 6:24), and worship His Father by exclaiming, "Thanks be unto God for his unspeakable gift!" (2 Cor. 9:15).

The Ultimate Benchmark for Self-Examination: Do We Love the Son of God?

Sincere love for the Lord Jesus Christ is always the crucial litmus test of religious experience. After all, love for God's Son is the mark of all marks of grace. That alone conclusively confirms that the love of the Father has truly been shed abroad in our hearts.

However, God's Word is equally clear that we cannot lay claim to loving the Lord Jesus Christ unless we demonstrate our love for Him by keeping His commandments. If we truly love the Living Word, the Father's beloved Son, we endeavor to honor Him by seek-ing to live in obedience to the written Word. True Christians always love the Scriptures precisely because they bear witness to the Living Word, Jesus Christ. This fully agrees with the love that functions within them, for He is the object of their love.

It should come as no surprise that the more we love and honor the Son, the more the Father is delighted—for the Father loves the Son! Jesus Himself testifies of this when He says, "He that loveth me shall be loved of my Father" (John 14:21). After all, the Father regen-erates sinners by His Spirit so that they might know, love, honor, and serve His Son. He wants His children to resemble His eternal Son in their disposition, words, and actions; He will not rest until, by His Spirit, they are conformed to the image of His Son. As we observed earlier, that is the great goal of predestination (Rom. 8:29).

The Wrath of God: Provoked by Those Who Do Not Love the Father's Son

If, then, the Father is eternally preoccupied with the Son of His love, has created all things for Him, and is redeeming sinners to become like Him, it follows that He neither can nor does tolerate anything that opposes His Son. The Father of the Lord Jesus Christ, who loves Him with an infinite love, can respond only with wrath against all who reject and oppose His beloved Son.

The wrath of God is the response of His whole holy being, in the totality of all His attributes, to the unbelieving rejection of His Son. The wrath of God is not one of His attributes per se; rather, it is the response of all of His attributes to those who hate His Son and reject His Word. Had there been no sin, there would have been no manifestation of God's wrath, for there would have been no occasion for it. However, man's sin, and particularly the unbelieving rejection of His Son, has provoked the Father to wrath—a wrath that is as infinite as His love for His Son. Nothing offends the Father more than our failure to love and honor the Son whom He loves.

There is thus a direct correlation between the love of the Father and His wrath. We could say that the wrath of the Father is the negative manifestation of the love He has for His Son. The intensity of His love for His Son demands the intensity of His wrath against all who hate and reject His Son—and especially against all who make Him a liar by not believing the record He has given of His Son in His Word (1 John 5:10). This is what prompted Paul to write, "If any man love not the Lord Jesus Christ, let him be Anathema [that is, accursed]!" (1 Cor. 16:22).

How fearful it will be for those who reject God's Son in unbelief to fall into the hands of the living God! How fearful to be confronted by the wrath of the Father who loves His Son (Heb. 10:31)! This explains the solemn admonition of the apostle, when he writes: "See that ye refuse not him that speaketh [the Living Word]. For if they escaped not who refused him that spake on earth [Moses], much more shall not we escape, if we turn away from him that speaketh from heaven [the Father's Son].... For our God is a consuming fire" (Heb. 12:25, 29). This also explains why immediately following our text (John 3:35), John the Baptist concludes his magnificent doxology about the Son by saying, "He that believeth not the Son shall not see life; but the wrath of God abideth on him" (v. 36).

This leads to an inescapable conclusion: the existence of hell has everything to do with the Father's love for His Son. Hell is created by the God whom John says is love—a love that has God's Son as its ultimate object! Hell is the Father's affirmation that He loves His Son—and that He loves Him so much that He will forever pour out His wrath upon all who hate Him. Hell is the only suitable and appropriate punishment for all who reject the Son.

This wrath will burn most intensely against those who lived under the gospel and to whom God's beloved Son, the Lord Jesus Christ, was freely offered. To be guilty of not having believed on this Christ, the Father's beloved Son, is the crime of all crimes! The Lord Jesus addressed this unbelieving rejection of the cities to whom He preached, saying:

> Woe unto thee, Chorazin! woe unto thee, Bethsaida! for if the mighty works, which were done in you, had been done in Tyre and Sidon, they would have repented long ago in sackcloth and ashes. But I say unto you, It shall be more tolerable for Tyre and Sidon at the day of judgment, than for you. And thou, Capernaum, which art exalted unto heaven, shalt be brought down to hell: for if the mighty works, which have been done in thee, had been done in Sodom, it would have remained until this day. But I say unto you, That it shall be more tolerable for the land of Sodom in the day of judgment, than for thee (Matt. 11:21–24).

The burning of God's wrath toward those who have rejected the Christ who was offered to them shall indeed be a hell in hell, for the Father loves His Son.

Conclusion

All of this makes the conclusion of Psalm 2 remarkable and fitting as a conclusion for this chapter: "Kiss the Son, lest he [the Father] be angry, and ye perish from the way, when his wrath is kindled but a little," for "blessed are all they that put their trust in him" (Ps. 2:12). May all of us trust in the Father's beloved Son alone for salvation, and may our lives confirm that we know, love, and serve this precious Christ.

May there also be a holy longing for the day when the Father will create a new heaven and a new earth by His Son and for His Son—the day of which Paul writes that the Father will "gather together in one all things in Christ, both which are in heaven, and which are on earth; even in him: in whom also we have obtained an inheritance, being predestinated according to the purpose of him who worketh all things after the counsel of his own will: that we should be to the praise of his glory, who first trusted in Christ" (Eph. 1:10–12).

May that blessed prospect cause us to pray with the church of all ages, "Come, Lord Jesus, come quickly." What a day that will be when the Father's beloved Son will present His beloved, blood-bought bride to His Father, and when the triune God and all true believers will celebrate the marriage supper of the Lamb forever! The adopted sons and daughters of the Father will forever dwell in that city of which it is written, "And the city had no need of the sun, neither of the moon, to shine in it: for the glory of God did lighten it, and the Lamb is the light thereof" (Rev. 21:23). That will be the day when the Father and His adopted children will delight themselves in the Son of His good pleasure, and forever He shall be all and in all!

CHAPTER 2

Father and Son in the Exodus

Jerry Bilkes

When Israel was a child, then I loved him,
and called my son out of Egypt.
—Hosea 11:1

In today's culture, there is a great deal of confusion about father-hood. Fatherhood, we could say, is in crisis. Millions of children live in homes where no father is present. Even in two-parent homes, many fathers are engulfed in busy lifestyles, so involved in their work, their hobbies, or their sports that they have no time for quality involvement in their children's lives. They may be physically present, but they are emotionally distant.

Fathers and children face tremendous communication chal-lenges today. Modern technology has given us the means to be in constant touch with one another, and yet its use often makes mean-ingful, face-to-face communication difficult. Imagine a busy father, always on his cell phone, even when he is in the car or at the park with his son. Search engines document the unhappy frequency of this question: "Why won't my dad talk to me?" Children feel shut out of their fathers' hearts and lives, misunderstood, and neglected. On the other hand, imagine a father trying to communicate with his son, who is constantly using his iPod with earbuds. The father feels unable to make his voice heard, unable to penetrate the clouds around his child.

In contrast to the mess that sinful humanity has made of father-hood, there is the fatherhood of God as it is revealed in the Scriptures. In this chapter, I aim to draw out a few aspects of the fatherhood of God as it is revealed in the Exodus and the history that followed the

Exodus, culminating in Jesus Christ's death on the cross and God's ongoing work of calling men and women to Himself.

Fatherhood in the Original Exodus
The critical passage that helps us see the fatherhood of God in the Exodus is found in Hosea 11:1: "When Israel was a child, then I loved him, and called my son out of Egypt." This verse refers to the exodus from Egypt, picturing it metaphorically in terms of a father and a son.

To understand this, we need to take a closer look at Egypt, the place of Israel's captivity. The Bible speaks a lot about Egypt, specifically, a lot about travel *into* and *out of* Egypt during the timeframe between about 2100 and 1400 BC. This comes as no surprise, for Egypt was the most dominant empire and power of that day. Armies, trade caravans, nomads, people looking to find anything from more food to a better future, and slaves being brought in to support the labor system would have been familiar sights along Egypt's border.

Somewhere around 2090 BC, perhaps lost in the crowds among the many caravans going in and out of Egypt, Abram, a Mesopotamian, one of the faithful, came into the land with a woman named Sarai, whom he called his half-sister, but who was actually his wife. Years later, he left again, a much richer man. Sometime later, around 1900 BC, a caravan of slave traders brought one of Abram's descendants, namely, Joseph, down into Egypt to be sold as a slave. Roughly twenty years later, the rest of Joseph's family came over the border into Egypt, where they grew to be a great nation and eventually were forced into slavery.

Then one day, the Egyptian crown prince, Moses, left the country, being led out by God for what we might call leadership training, a time of preparation for what would happen on a special night forty years in the future. This was the night when, with a heavy hand, God brought two million or so of the descendants of Abram (or Abraham) out of bondage in Egypt to freedom. Whether or not the other comings and goings of God's people over this border had been noticed or deemed significant by men of this world, this mass exodus certainly was. What a sight it must have been! Egypt's border has undoubtedly been a witness to God's providential leadings and to the gradual unfolding of His redemptive plan. His people's comings and goings over that border were very significant.

It was especially the bondage that the Israelites experienced there that gave Egypt its significance in the Bible. Egypt came to symbolize the power of darkness, which holds down the people of God and tries to destroy them. It could be seen as a symbol of satanic power, of Satan, the ancient serpent, whose design it was to destroy the seed of the woman (Gen. 3:15). Think of how the Israelite baby boys were thrown into the Nile River according to Pharaoh's commandment (Ex. 1:22). Wasn't that Satan's work? Yet, as God had promised, the serpent would not succeed. In fact, his plans would have to serve the purposes of God. The Nile that should have destroyed the seed was the same river that delivered Moses, the future redeemer of the people, right into Pharaoh's household, where he would be educated by Pharaoh's daughter (2:1–10).

When Pharaoh finally turned against Moses, God called Moses out of Egypt as a pattern for what would happen with the whole nation forty years later. To use a different picture, Moses left first as the head of the body (namely, Israel), but soon afterward, the body itself could not but follow.

All of this was put into the metaphor of a father and son when God said, "Israel is my son, even my firstborn" (Ex. 4:22). To Pharaoh, Moses was told to say, "Let my son go, that he may serve me: and if thou refuse to let him go, behold, I will slay thy son, even thy firstborn" (v. 23). In the Exodus, God was calling His son, His firstborn, out of captivity, in order that the Israelites would be free to serve Him, their Father, in the wilderness.

This would be the most noteworthy coming or going from Egypt yet. God's call brought about the freedom of the son. How powerful the voice of God is! His call drew His son irresistibly. Even when Israel resisted its own freedom by murmuring and complaining against Moses, God's call prevailed, and Israel came out. The exodus was an important day for the nation. Before this time, the Israelites were servants or minors, as Paul says, "in bondage" and "under tutors and governors" (Gal. 4:2–3). The exodus was their great redemption. We could say that the exodus was Israel's coming of age—the day when the people were presented to the world as the adult son of God, serving Him as His heir.

What a picture the Bible gives of the fatherhood of God in the exodus. Here is an alternative to the confusion today. Here we have a Father who involves Himself with His son. He cares deeply about His son, and delights in him. He delivers him from bondage with His powerful call. His call brings about a change in His son's life that brings him onto the stage of history as a free, grown son, ready to serve his Father. What an identity this gave the Israelites. They were the precious children of God, called into the freedom of a life of service to their gracious Father.

Fatherhood in the Decisive Exodus

Perhaps you know the saying that though *Israel* was taken out of *Egypt*, this did not mean that *Egypt* was taken out of *Israel*. As the Israelites left Egypt, never to return, they took "Egypt" with them. From early on in their national history, they showed themselves to be a less-than-ideal son of such a gracious and redeeming Father. Over and over, they needed to be called away from living as Egypt lived, worshiping as Egypt worshiped, and thinking as Egypt thought.

It took only a few days for Israel to show its true colors after its exodus from Egypt. The people murmured against the Lord, provoked Him by worshiping the golden calf, and showed themselves to have unbelieving and hard hearts. After they entered the Promised Land, they continued to stray from their Father. The Lord often called them back to himself, with warnings and threatenings, but also with gracious promises about a coming Savior who would be what they could never be of themselves—the Son of God.

Take what Hosea says about Israel: "They sacrificed unto Baalim, and burned incense to graven images" (11:2). This is one of the reasons that Hosea reminds them, "I...called my son out of Egypt" (v. 1b). The prophet wanted to remind the people of this truth: having been called out of Egypt in the past, they had no business living like Egypt in the present. They had not been living as the people of God. Instead, they were "bent to backsliding from me" (v. 7). From painful personal experience, Hosea understood how deeply rooted the ways of Egypt were in the hearts of God's people. Incredibly, they seemed bent on returning to bondage. And, he said, that was indeed where they were headed—not back to the land of Egypt, but "the Assyrian shall be his king" (v. 5). The people of God would be exiled into bondage in Assyria and Babylon. Yet they would not be destroyed. There they would stay, Hosea said, until the Lord called them again out of "Egypt." That call, Hosea said, would be more like a roar: "He shall roar like a lion: when he shall roar, then the children shall tremble from the west. They shall tremble as a bird out of Egypt, and as a dove out of the land of Assyria: and I will place them in their houses, saith the LORD" (vv. 10b–11).

The return of the exiles to their native land would be a first fulfillment of the prophet Hosea's words. Yet, as is often the case in Old Testament prophecy, a greater and deeper fulfillment would follow. All would not be well after the people were allowed to return to their land. Their troubles would not all be behind them. Sin would still show itself among the people of God. Idolatry would still rear its head. They would need a more spiritual, more spectacular, more decisive exodus.

In our Bibles, we need to turn forward only about fifty pages, from Hosea to the book of Matthew, to see this begin to happen decisively. We can find Hosea's own words quoted there: "Out of Egypt have I called my son" (Matt. 2:15). As they are fulfilled there, they take on a deeper, more amazing significance.

Matthew writes of the time when the Lord Jesus, the Savior, was a young child. After the wise men had visited this King of the Jews, because of the threat of Herod, Joseph, Mary's husband, "took the young child and his mother by night, and departed into Egypt: and was there until the death of Herod: that it might be fulfilled which was spoken of the Lord by the prophet, saying, Out of Egypt have I called my son" (Matt. 2:14–15).

It is interesting to see the parallels between this time in history and the period preceding the first exodus. Then, it was Pharaoh trying to destroy the seed of the woman; later, it is Herod trying to destroy the seed of the woman. This is taking place not in Egypt but in Israel itself, in Bethlehem, the birthplace of David and of Christ. Then the baby boys were thrown into the Nile; later, they are killed with the swords of Herod's soldiers. But even though some of the particulars are different, the underlying themes are the same and, in fact, intensified. In Matthew, we are dealing specifically with *the* seed of the woman. And in Matthew, Egypt is not the enemy, but the enemy is *within Israel itself,* on the throne of the nation whom God had chosen. In fact, quite remarkably, Egypt is the place where the seed of the woman, the divine Redeemer, finds shelter and protection from Herod, much like Pharaoh's daughter sheltered and protected the redeemer Moses. Obviously, these parallels are not coincidences.

Imagine the night when Mary, Joseph, and the young child Jesus set out to return home. Would they have caught your attention as they crossed the Egyptian border that night? Perhaps you have seen scenes like this, a family trying to leave one country in order to reach another. Had you seen them, you might have wondered, where is that family going? What will life in a new country be like for them? Will they find a better life? What will become of the child? Will He grow up and make something of Himself? Little could anyone who watched Mary, Joseph, and Jesus cross the border out of Egypt that night have known that this child with a humble couple would change all of history.

That evening at the border marked the critical transition from despair to hope, from bondage to freedom, and from persecution to protection in the divine plan for human history. That child would not only influence His own country, but He would open the gates of heaven and defeat the forces of hell, orchestrating an incredible exodus from sin and its tyranny in human hearts everywhere.

So when a plain-looking Jewish couple with a toddler left the country one night shortly after Herod's death, none around them recognized it, but God called it an exodus. In fact, Jesus was fulfilling the exodus, as Matthew points out: "That it might be *fulfilled*" (v. 15).

How fitting it was that no pomp or circumstance attended Jesus that night as He came out of Egypt. After all, there was none to accompany His birth, either. That would prove to be how things would go in this Son's life. There would be no pomp and circumstance during His childhood in humble Nazareth, or as He started His work in carpentry. As He began His ministry, He would go unnoticed by many, attracting the most attention from those who envied and despised Him. Even when Moses and Elijah came to speak to Him on the Mount of Transfiguration about His approaching death (which, interestingly, the original text also calls an "exodus"), only three disciples were present as eyewitnesses. There would especially be no pomp and circumstance when Christ would ultimately descend into the Egypt of death on the cross of Calvary. Yet, there on the cross, through His passion and death, He would work a redemption infinitely greater than anything that happened in the first exodus. In His death as the Firstborn of His people, He would accomplish a second and superior exodus. He did it all that He "might destroy him that had the power of death, that is, the devil; and deliver them who through fear of death were all their lifetime subject to bondage" (Heb. 2:14b–15).

Christ's obedience to His Father's call continued throughout His life on earth. The Son's ears were always open to the Father's voice. The communication between them was never challenged. The Son always heard His Father (Isa. 50:4) and did what pleases Him (John 8:29). We could say that the Son's ear was always perfectly tuned to the Father's voice. Where the Father said He should go, He went. What the Father said He should do, He did. On the cross, things were no different. We read in John: "Therefore doth my Father love me, because I lay down my life, that I might take it again…. This commandment have I received of my Father" (John 10:17–18).

On the cross, Christ heard and obeyed the call of the Father, and in His very last breath, He, as it were, stepped toward His Father, over the finishing line at the border of Egypt, with the cry, "It is finished" (John 19:30). The Father took hold of the Son, and the Son placed His life into the hand of the Father with the words, "Into thine hand I commit my spirit: thou hast redeemed me, O LORD God of truth" (Ps. 31:5; cf. Luke 23:46). And the Father, reverently speaking, took the spirit of the Son. Then He raised Him up on the third day, before principalities and powers in heavenly places, and, exulting in the glory of the resurrection, He said, as it were, in triumph: "Out of Egypt I have called My Son. See it, devil. You tried to swallow Him up, but here He is with the power of an endless life, having conquered death, hell, and the grave. He is My Son, My Servant, My Heir, My First-begotten from the dead, and Prince of the kings of the earth."

Do you see why the exodus of the young Christ from Egypt was a decisive one? Rather than staying in forced exile in Egypt because of Herod's envy, Christ was called back by His Father, to grow up and begin His ministry, and finally to suffer and die in obedience to His Father's call. His perfect service to His Father in all of these things purchased for His people a decisive exodus, which He would unpack and apply in an ongoing exodus.

Fatherhood in the Ongoing Exodus
This call of the Father to the Son has resounded down through the centuries, effecting an ongoing exodus. It is closely tied to the second exodus, for Christ as Head has accomplished the redemption and is applying it to His body, His people, bringing them out of a spiritual Egypt still today. At the very heart of this exodus is the Father, who is still effectually calling His people, enslaved to sin and Satan, out of their bondage and into His service, and along the way showing His true Father heart, from which we can and must learn at various levels of our lives.

What can we say about this Fatherly call?

1. It is a powerful call. God says that He *calls* His Son out of Egypt. I noted above that many fathers today are not communicating meaningfully with their children. Yet this Father not only speaks, He *calls.* A call is different from a statement. It is a directive that comes with power. It is an exhortation that demands a response. Fathers are often weak and insipid; we have trouble speaking with authority and getting a response. But this Father is strong, and His words effect change.

How does God call today? He sends forth messengers of the gospel, who say: "Come out of Egypt. Come out of the darkness." Many are content in the darkness, and the devil works hard to keep them there. Yet just as powerfully as God brought His people out of Egypt in the original exodus, so He powerfully draws His people today. No power on earth or even in hell is able to keep God's call from effecting this great change.

2. It is an uncovering call. God's call is to a people in Egypt. Just as it did to the Israelites in Egypt, God's call uncovers and unmasks the forces of bondage, as well as the heart that clings to bondage. It even evokes the murmuring and unbelief that many exhibit when they hear the call of God in the Egypt of sin. Thereby this call unmasks to us our bondage and inability to free ourselves.

3. It is a drawing call. Hosea 11:3–4 and 8–9 picture the drawing power of God's love beautifully. The cords that He uses are cords of lovingkindness or covenant love. Gently and yet effectually, the

Lord woos His son out of Egypt. Calvary is the proof of that love; from Calvary that call is heard with power. Calvary calls out that there is a way of escape through the blood of the Firstborn, Jesus Christ, the Son of God. But this call also makes clear that if you stay in Egypt, you can anticipate only more and more misery. Because God's eternal Son went into the Egypt of death on the cross, there is a way out of Egypt for sinners. The call is not: "Make the payment yourself—shed your own blood as a ransom." No, it is this: "Christ, the Redeemer, has shed His blood." God called His Son out of Egypt in the cross and resurrection. By the Spirit, God applies the blood to sinners, and His Word of the cross brings them out of bondage.

4. *It is a call that begets faith.* This Father challenges His son to a bold, transformed life, and God's call actually provides the very faith that is necessary. Coming out of Egypt involves trust and reliance on God, following where He leads. It is not always easy to understand why the Father leads us where He does, but we are called to trust Him even when we do not understand His dealings. God's people often seem to have a hard trek through this wilderness. We still find Egypt at our elbows and much of Egypt still in our hearts. Nevertheless, the Father's call works on our hearts in order to fan the flame of faith, which brings us to rely more and more on our Head, the Redeemer, Christ Jesus.

5. *It is a call to separation and service.* Many fathers today are reluctant to tell their children what to do. However, this Father's call comes with an identity and obligation. Israel was called out of Egypt in order to serve God as His son in the wilderness. So, too, God's people are delivered in order to serve the Lord as His sons and daughters. They find themselves out of place in this world, more like people going through a wilderness, but they are with their Father and they are His children. They have an identity that separates them and sanctifies them. We need grace to tell the world that we are not here to be like them, but to serve our God and our Father.

6. *It is an urgent call.* I have been emphasizing the border of Egypt. You are either in Egypt or not in Egypt. It's that simple. One step separates the two. One inch from the border, you are still in Egypt. But one inch beyond the border, you are outside of Egypt. "I...called my son out of Egypt," God says. It is not sufficient to be only among the professing people of God; it's possible to be among the professing

people of God and still be in Egypt. To be in Egypt means to be under the power of darkness and the control of sin, living, as Paul says, under the rudiments of the world, including religious codes and works of human righteousness (see Gal. 4:1–4).

I began by referring to the fatherhood crisis in our culture today. Many young people are complaining that their fathers will not talk to them. But we have a Father that not only talks, He calls, and His call gives identity and liberty. Still today He says with delight and pleasure in the hearts of His people, "I…called my son out of Egypt." Do we have ears to hear this call?

This exodus is going on still today, but one day it will be over. God is bringing His people in His Son across the border of Egypt, and a countless number have already come over. Believers now live in the wilderness of this world, but one day they will sing the song of Moses and the Lamb (Rev. 15:3). I pray that none of you will be omitted from that innumerable company, those who have been called out of Egypt into the sonship and heirship of God through Jesus Christ, God's Son.

ADORING THE BEAUTIFUL ATTRIBUTES OF THE FATHER

CHAPTER 3

The Holiness of the Father in the Old Testament

Derek W. H. Thomas

Isaiah 6

Isaiah 6 is a very familiar passage, so familiar that many could recite the opening verses from memory. Many Christians have regarded it as a vision of the pre-incarnate Christ. Even the apostle John supports that view. Isaiah, John informs us, "saw his glory, and spake of him" (John 12:41), referring to Jesus.

But there is perhaps something of a problem. When we read the Old Testament from the point of view of the New Testament, we can see what no Jew—not Moses, David, Isaiah, Ezekiel, or Daniel—ever saw: the doctrine of the Trinity! We may read God's words in the account of creation, "Let us make man in our image, after our likeness" (Gen. 1:26), and see that the plural pronoun ("us") is perfectly harmonious with the fact that there is deliberation within the Trinity: the Father and the Son are in communication together, deliberating on the creation of Adam and Eve. But Moses did not draw any such conclusion. In fact, no Jew ever suggested that there exists plurality within the *one* God. That should give us pause and temper our over-zealous attempts to read too much into the Old Testament. Standard Jewish interpretation viewed the plural use of God's name (*Elohim*) and the use of "us" in Genesis 1:26 as a plurality of reverence rather than a plurality of "persons."

Therefore, it is a mistake to read John 12:41 and to then go back to Isaiah 6 and say, "This is all about Jesus." Actually, this is a revelation of God. As John Calvin writes in his commentary on Isaiah:

> Who was that Lord? John tells us it was Christ, (John xii.41) and justly, for God never revealed himself to the Fathers but in his

eternal Word and only begotten Son. Yet it is wrong, I think, to limit this, as some do, to the person of Christ.… In this passage, therefore, God is mentioned indefinitely, and yet it is correctly said that Isaiah saw the glory of Christ, for at that very time he was *the image of the invisible God* (Col. i.15).[1]

So, Isaiah 6 is as much a revelation of the Father as of the Son.

The Death of an Earthly King

There is deep significance in the preamble to this chapter: "In the year that king Uzziah died" (Isa. 6:1a). It recounts the death of a once notable and significant earthly king. He had a long reign of fifty-two years. Isaiah has already been called as a prophet, though that call will be renewed in this chapter. He had ministered, therefore, during Uzziah's reign, and has cause to ponder the downfall of such a great man and the consequences that might follow for the people of God.

Tiglath-Pileser III, the great Assyrian king and to some extent imperialist, had arisen and is threatening the existence of the northern kingdom, which has its capital in Samaria. Isaiah is a long way from Samaria; he is in Jerusalem, in the southern kingdom. But he is warning the kings of the southern kingdom about the threat that Assyria (and later Babylon) poses to Jerusalem.

Uzziah was a good king until the end, when he did something that was a violation of God's commandments. The story is recounted in 2 Chronicles 26. King Uzziah usurped the role of the high priest, entering into the Holy Place and offering incense to the Lord. God struck him with leprosy, and he lived out his days in a leper colony outside the city. Perhaps his family visited and left food, but they could not go near him. It was a tragic way for a great king to end his days.

Now he is dead. Perhaps Isaiah is pondering these things in the temple precincts, the very place where the king had violated God's command and where the first signs of leprosy had become evident on his skin. Then Isaiah sees a vision of God, glorious and terrible. The earthly king is dead, but the King of kings is very much alive. The earthly king is dead, but God is on His throne.

Isaiah sees an appearance of God, a *theophany*—a manifestation of God in visible form. In the temple, Isaiah meets God as he has

---

1. John Calvin, *Calvin's Commentaries*, 22 vols., Vol. VII: *Commentary on the Book of the Prophet Isaiah*, trans. William Pringle (Grand Rapids: Baker, 1981), 201.

never met Him before. At once, he is overcome by the sheer majesty, mystery, and immensity of the scene. God comes to the prophet to reveal something about His character, about the way that He is. It is a vision of God in majesty.

Four elements in this passage warrant attention: first, the vision of the holiness of God; second, the vision of God's judgment; third, the vision of God's grace; and fourth, the imperative on Isaiah as a consequence of this vision—the commission.

Holiness

Isaiah receives revelation in both his eyes and ears. He hears the sound of seraphim singing the so-called *trisagion*, "Holy, holy, holy, is the LORD of hosts" (Isa. 6:3). The covenant God of Israel, the God of armies, the mighty God, is, in the words of Alec Motyer, "the super superlatively holy One."[2]

Holiness in the Old Testament has two meanings or origins. One is *purity*—brightness and shining. Another meaning, the most predominant in the Old Testament, is the idea of *separation*. In the Old Testament era, all kinds of things were said to be holy, even such things as pots and pans, spoons, knives, forks, ladles, and all kinds of kitchenware. They were holy because they were used for special purposes in the temple. There was nothing particularly different about them *per se*; they were different because they were categorized as "made for this *only*."

God is revealing Himself here in a category that is altogether different. It is a category that belongs to Himself. It is hard to pigeonhole or categorize God. We speak of God by analogy because He is different from us. He is the Creator; we are just creatures. We know things, but God knows things in a way that is altogether different from the way we know them. We know things discursively. We know things because we reason from A to B to C to D. But God knows everything all at once. He is infinite, eternal, unchangeable in His being, wisdom, power, holiness, justice, goodness, and truth.[3] God is giving His prophet an audio-visual display of His being, His character, His holiness, His separateness, and His distinctiveness.

---

2. Alec Motyer, *Look to the Rock: An Old Testament Background to our Understanding of Christ* (Leicester, England: IVP, 1996), 67.
3. Westminster Shorter Catechism, Q. 4.

He does it *spatially*. Isaiah sees God high and lifted up. I do not know how tall Isaiah was, but we have to imagine him as peering up and up, seeing this vision of the holiness and immensity of God. God is high and lifted up. This is a way of explaining the exalted character of God. God is not on our plane.

The revelation of God in the Old Testament is intimidating. There is something about this vision that says God is unapproachable. We need to stay well back! It is the glory of the gospel, the dawning of the fullness of times when Christ comes, that we may come into the presence of God and call Him, "Abba, Father" (Rom. 8:15; Gal. 4:6). No Jew ever dared to do that. There are little glimpses here and there where we see God addressed as Father, but they are sparse. But with the coming of Christ in the New Testament, there is a much fuller, richer revelation of God as our heavenly Father. However, that revelation is not here. Here, the picture of God is intimidating. He is high and lifted up. We can almost sense the way in which the prophet is crushed with the smallness of mankind in comparison to the greatness and unfathomability of God.

The vision is described *geologically*. The ground begins to shake: "And the posts of the door moved at the voice of him that cried" (v. 4a). I have experienced earthquakes twice. There was something uncanny about the building slowly rocking back and forth— so uncanny that on both occasions I felt the need to evacuate the building! Isaiah finds himself in what feels like an earthquake, and perhaps he has an equally strong desire to leave the building. God is unmanageable. When He comes, the ground shakes.

The vision is also described *sensationally*: Isaiah cannot breathe because the temple fills with smoke (v. 4b). As I write these lines, my neighbor's house sits empty because it caught fire. I looked out of my study window to see black smoke and fire emerging from its roof. Likewise, in the vision, the temple seems to be on fire. God has come in His holiness and the building is ablaze.

The vision is also described *psychologically* and *spiritually*. Isaiah senses something of his own unworthiness. Holy seraphs, "burning ones" who have never sinned and know nothing of guilt, are covering themselves in the presence of God (v. 2). They have six wings, and they cover their faces and bodies (covering their feet implies that their bodies are also covered). These holy creatures have never sinned, but they cannot bear to look upon the intimidating presence of Almighty God. The holiness of God causes them to hide. In their creatureliness, they are overcome by the presence of God.

Judgment

There is something intimidating about God even to sinless creatures. They, too, must acknowledge their place as part of His creation and offer to serve Him with all of their being. With two wings they fly, ready to go wherever God sends them. They view their role as one of service. They exist to do His bidding.

But for Isaiah, it is worse, *much* worse than that. The holiness of God for a sinner can mean only one thing—*judgment*. He cries, "Woe is me! for I am undone; because I am a man of unclean lips, and I dwell in the midst of a people of unclean lips" (v. 5). Surely not! Isaiah? He is one of godliest of the prophets, a man used by God to preach to kings and prophesy of the coming of Jesus. Surely Isaiah has the most pure lips in Israel. Why, then, is he saying, "I am a man of unclean lips"? He speaks of himself as "undone" by this experience, for God's gaze has pierced his very soul and torn him asunder. If this is true of Isaiah, what hope can there be for the rest of us?

Sin warrants only one response—judgment. And when we catch a glimpse of the sin in our hearts, the holiness of God threatens to unhinge us. This was my experience at the close of 1971 when I read the Bible for the first time. I had never considered who God was in any serious way before, but when I came to examine Him as He reveals Himself in Scripture, I, too, was undone. I knew myself to be a sinner and, apart from grace, deserving only of condemnation and hell. That is what holiness does.

The church has lost sight of the holiness of God. For far too many, God is a little bit like "Jeeves" in the P. G. Wodehouse books—a somewhat eccentric butler, ready to do our bidding. God is not Santa Claus. He is not some doting grandfather who is nice and kind. The God and Father of our Lord Jesus Christ reveals Himself in such a way that the only response the prophet can give is, "Woe is me! for I am undone; because I am a man of unclean lips."

It is very interesting that Isaiah should mention his lips. He is, after all, one who speaks for a living. The point at which he senses his sin the greatest is the point of his greatest usefulness. It is true of us all. Our most sinful acts are usually in the very calling that God has given to us. At the point of greatest grace, we see the greatest ingratitude on our part.

Do you, I wonder, know anything about your sin? Does it disturb you enough to make you want to run from God's presence and say, "All my righteousness is *as filthy rags*" (Isa. 64:6)? Remember, Isaiah made this discovery as a believer who had been in service to God for some years! "Some Christians," Sinclair Ferguson writes, "never seem to make this discovery about themselves. They are never brought to the place where they see that it is their 'strengths' or 'qualities' or 'gifts' that stand in need of cleansing from God. No discovery could be more devastating. *And if the sense of the presence of the Holy One does anything, it devastates a man or a woman.*"[4] Do you know anything of this devastation? Have you experienced the holiness of God in this way?

Grace

As soon as Isaiah acknowledges his wretchedness, there is a display of extraordinary grace—and grace is always extraordinary! A seraph is seen flying with a live coal (Isa. 6:6), a coal he has taken from the altar of sacrifice, where victims are killed and burnt as offerings.

We need to notice how Isaiah 6 begins and ends with death, what we sometimes refer to as an *inclusio*. It begins with the death of Uzziah and ends with a picture of a tree that has been felled. It is a dead tree. From this death, life will come. Notice, too, that the live coal from the altar reminds us of death—the death of a sacrificial victim, a substitute who has met the holiness of God and died. In a graphic display of atonement and justification, a live coal now touches Isaiah's lips—the very place where he has expressed his sin.

When you feel utterly condemned, when you are conscious of having broken God's law, and when you are unhinged by the reality of His holiness, His purity, His justice, His sovereignty, His otherness, His absolute distinction from you, what a glorious thing it is to know there is forgiveness with God, that He may be feared!

Martin Luther once said, describing his own narrative of a surprising conversion, "I feel as though I have begun to be dissolved in the presence of God." When that happens to Isaiah, God comes

---

4. Sinclair Ferguson, *A Heart for God* (Edinburgh: Banner of Truth, 1987), 87.

with a word of forgiveness, touches his mouth, and says, "Lo, this hath touched thy lips; and thine iniquity is taken away, and thy sin purged" (v. 7).

What does it take to forgive sin? God does not spare His own Son, but freely offers Him up as a sacrifice for us, in our place. Nicholas Wolterstorff, a Christian philosopher, wrote a little book, *Lament for a Son*, after his son fell to his death in a climbing accident. He was in his early twenties. Wolterstorff describes this in his book. When he speaks to audiences, he is asked, "How should we introduce you?" Wolterstorff says, "I am a father who has lost a son." He says that that loss defines him. Not a day goes by but that is how he thinks about himself—as a father who has lost a son.[5]

Our heavenly Father has, in a sense, lost a Son. He knows what it is to lose an only Son. Jesus cried out, "My God, my God, why hast thou forsaken me?" (Mark 15:34). In the cry of dereliction on the cross, Jesus did not say, "My Father, my Father," but "My God, my God." It was as though the assurance of His native sonship had been obliterated because of imputed sin and guilt. All that He was conscious of was being the greatest sinner that the world had ever seen. He was conscious of being in the place of the wicked—damned, forsaken, and abandoned. God did not spare Him but freely delivered Him up for us all. *That* is the gospel. The Holy Father has only one Son, and He gave Him up for us. Do not interpret the atonement as though Jesus was trying to arm-wrestle a reluctant heavenly Father. That is an atrocity! That is not the gospel; that is not the atonement of Scripture. God so loved the world that He gave His only begotten Son. This Holy Father, this righteous God, this pure being who cannot look upon sin, gives to the prophet this picture of atonement.

Commission

Following the vision, God calls the prophet to service, saying, "Whom shall I send, and who will go for us?" Isaiah's response is immediate and definitive: "Here am I; send me" (v. 8). This is not the first call that Isaiah has received. He is given a glimpse of the gospel in a fresh way, and the sight of it impels him into ministry with renewed zeal and conviction. We need to experience the gospel every day. We need to *preach the gospel to ourselves every day*.

---

5. Nicholas Wolterstorff, *Lament for a Son* (Grand Rapids: Eerdmans, 1987).

But what is Isaiah's calling? To what does the holiness of God impel him? The answer is both humbling and disturbing. He is sent on *Mission: Impossible.* We see this in verses 9–13: "Go, and tell this people...." Tell them what? In effect, he is told: "Isaiah, I'm going to call you to be the most successful preacher the world has ever seen, and tens of thousands, no, millions of people are going to come to hear you. You will be a televangelist, and your face will be broadcast all over the world. You will have success like you cannot begin to imagine."

God's call says nothing of the kind, of course. His mission is going to be largely unfruitful. This is a time of judgment in Israel's history. Assyria will come, and after Assyria, Babylon, and then exile. There will be two hundred years and more of dark days, and then even after the exile it will still be a day of relatively small things. Although the people will rebuild the temple, it will not be the same as before. The ark of the covenant will be gone. The very symbol of the presence of God will be lost.

There are dark days ahead, and Isaiah is called to proclaim a message that says, "You are not going to be very successful." Imagine that. Imagine being called to proclaim a message, knowing in advance that your message isn't going to be very successful. It is only going to confirm the people in their willful stubbornness of unbelief. But God doesn't call us to be successful; He calls us to be faithful.

"Who will go for us?" Who wants God's commission? Who wants His calling? Who wants to spend the rest of their lives doing what Isaiah is being called to do here? Isaiah says, "Here am I; send me."

Where is God calling *you* to go? What is God calling you to do? You have experienced the Father's holy love and atonement that cost the death of His Son, an unimaginable cost! Where is He calling you to go, and where are you going in your home, in your family, with your children, in your vocation, in your church? Are you prepared to say, "Here am I; send me; I'll do it; I'll go"?

CHAPTER 4

The Father's Mercy

William VanDoodewaard

> *Blessed be the God and Father of our Lord Jesus Christ, which accord-*
> *ing to his abundant mercy hath begotten us again unto a lively hope by*
> *the resurrection of Jesus Christ from the dead, to an inheritance incor-*
> *ruptible, and undefiled, and that fadeth not away, reserved in heaven*
> *for you, who are kept by the power of God through faith unto salvation*
> *ready to be revealed in the last time.*
>
> —1 Peter 1:3–5

Do you ever feel discouraged, fearful, or lonely in your Christian life? Peter's epistle was written to a people facing discouragement under the pressures of hostility and persecution—"the strangers [or 'exiles'] scattered throughout…" (1 Peter 1:1). Why did he call them strangers or exiles? Because their neighbors, coworkers, and society at large thought it strange that the Christians did not run with them in head-long pursuit of lusts, drunkenness, wild parties, and idolatries. They spoke evil of the Christians because they did not join in these things. They spoke evil of Christ, of God. To this people the apostle writes, "if any man suffer as a Christian, let him not be ashamed" (4:16).

Our great God, our Lord Jesus Christ, gives profound encour-agement through the apostle Peter to an ostracized and discouraged people—a people "in heaviness through manifold temptations" (1:6)—in 1 Peter 1:3–5. This passage gives the solution to fears and pressures by shifting our focus to see, know, and worship God the Father as we come to know Him better, and to know what He has done and is doing in His great mercy for us. We see this in two parts: first, in what the Father has done for us and why (vv. 3–4), and sec-ond, in what the Father is doing for us and why (v. 5).

What the Father Has Done (1 Peter 1:3–4)

In these verses, Peter is bursting into worship and praise of God the Father, full of enthusiastic love and thankfulness. He is overflowing with gratitude: "Blessed be the God and Father of our Lord Jesus Christ." Why is Peter's heart filled with praise? It is because God the Father, in His abundant mercy, has given new life and new status in Christ to him and to the believers he is addressing. God the Father has acted "according to his abundant mercy." How? He has "begotten us again," or, to put it in more current language, has "caused us to be born again." John Calvin comments that we are all "born children of wrath"; yet, in great mercy, the Father "rebirths us" by His Word and Spirit, in and through His only begotten Son, so that we become His children. The terms "born again" and "begotten" carry the implication of sonship. You and I were born as children of the parents who bore and birthed us. What a mystery, what an incredible transformation and blessing God's Word declares here! It is the privilege of being rebirthed as the sons of God when we were rebel creatures!

Another word that Scripture uses to describe our "born-again" status as children of the Father is "adoption"; Romans 8:14–16 uses the term "adoption" in describing the fruit of being "born again" by the Spirit of God. Paul makes clear that the new birth worked by the Spirit not only brings us back into the presence, fellowship, and fatherhood of God, but through it we are transformed into the children of God: "As many as are led by the Spirit of God, they are the sons of God. For ye have not received the spirit of bondage again to fear; but ye have received the Spirit of adoption, whereby we cry, Abba, Father!" We become God's children, so that we now increasingly love, know, obey, and honor God the Father as our Father. As His children, we can call out to Him, "Abba, Father; dear Father!" What a change in relationship! We, all believers, were condemned, dead sinners, hard criminals facing the holy justice of God. But now, you and I who are born again in Christ are children of God the Father. We have been brought by the triune God through Jesus' atoning work to forever share in Jesus' relationship to the Father! So, people of God, God the Father is your Father. He is perfectly kind and tender, knowing your frailties. His only begotten Son, Jesus Christ, is now your elder brother. All this has happened through His service as the perfect Mediator and eternal High Priest.

Why does God speak this to us by His Word? Why is He telling us this? He wants us to know Him, trust Him, and enjoy Him as our Father! Does your heart resonate with this? Do you live aware, in wonder and worship as a child, of God the Father as *your* Father? If you are in Christ, this is yours: God the Father is your Father. Join with Peter in rejoicing in and worshiping Him—you are children of the Father.

Do not allow sin to constrict your heart and mind to think miserly thoughts of Him when He is a Father of abundant mercy! Do not allow sin to dull you, to separate you from your Father who has "rebirthed" you, caused you to be born again. Do not excuse a lack of intimate communion with your Father in heaven through a false humility, as if your unworthiness presents an insurmountable barrier: your Father has freely given at infinite cost. He has done everything for your salvation and eternal blessing by the gift of His eternal Son, done everything to do away with the barrier of your sin, and as your Father He freely lavishes on you everything that you need for sweet fellowship with Him.

At the same time, if, in thinking back on your life, you realize that you have never known the Father as your Father, that you have never been filled with love and wonder toward Him, then you desperately need to realign your life and theology with His Word. You need to come to Christ to receive grace and life, new birth. It is Christ's delight, as well as His sovereign ministry and mission, to redeem and save men, women, and children from sinful alienation to new birth, to new life as sons of the Father. He brings us to know the Father—just as He is seen to be doing by His Word in 1 Peter.

It is this connection to the Father by and in Christ that Peter goes on to declare to us as the people of God in the latter part of verse 3: "God the Father hath begotten us [or 'caused us to be born again']... by [or 'through'] the resurrection of Jesus Christ from the dead." Our new birth, our new life as children of God, is the result of Jesus' death and resurrection. You who are mothers know by experience, and fathers by seeing, that giving birth is costly. It is a tremendous sacrifice of life energy and effort. It is painful and hard—agonizing. Birth involves suffering and shedding blood. This is perhaps one of the closest earthly illustrations of the costliness of being born again.

God the Father, who has caused us to be born again, did so knowing that rebirthing and adopting us would not be cheap. It was infinitely more costly than any human birth. We were bought with the price of the lifeblood, the wrath-bearing sufferings to death of the eternal, only begotten Son of the Father! As believers, we were birthed to new life through the agony of Christ's suffering: His bloodshed. And the very power of God that rebirthed us, that keeps us in new life, living and growing as children of the Father, is the same power by which Jesus was raised from the dead.

You see, Jesus' resurrection is proof of the completion of His sacrifice for our sin, and it also shows the power that He has to save and preserve, to sanctify and to glorify; a power given to Him by the Father. As Revelation 5:12 says, "Worthy is the Lamb that was slain to receive power, and riches, and wisdom, and strength, and honour, and glory, and blessing." First Corinthians 1:24 tells us that "Christ [is] the power of God, and the wisdom of God." God gives "the exceeding greatness of his power to us-ward who believe" (Eph. 1:19). It is this invincible atonement–sealing resurrection power of Jesus Christ and of God the Father that has begotten us, causing us to be "born again" to new, eternal life as the children of God! The Spirit tells us by the Word that this is what gives a "lively" or "living" hope to the Christian—a lively confidence, a trust that is alive, living faith in God as our Father, contentment in the certainty of His promises, and a sure hope for the future, a hope that is alive.

Why Has the Father Done This?

The second blessing that Peter describes is the future inheritance that God has provided for us as His children: "To [obtain] an inheritance incorruptible, and undefiled, and that fadeth not away, reserved in heaven for you" (v. 4). We are born again, made children of the Father, for a glorious purpose. We see that we are born again not only to a "living hope," but also "to an inheritance." Remember again the context of the first recipients of this letter: they were scattered and persecuted, and their persecution often included job losses, financial hardships, and earthly poverty. Now they receive news reminding them that they are to receive an inheritance.

What is this inheritance? Verse 5 gives some direction: our inheritance as the children of God is related to the "salvation ready to be revealed in the last time." Scripture often speaks of the inheritance of the children of God. The Lord said to Aaron in Numbers 18:20,

"Thou shalt have no inheritance in their land, neither shalt thou have any part among them: I am thy part and thine inheritance among the children of Israel." In his priestly role, Aaron pictured the better inheritance that was to come.

The book of Revelation, perhaps most of all the New Testament books, describes the inheritance of the children of the Father. Ours is the new Jerusalem, the heavenly city, and the new heaven and the new earth, but most of all, central to all, our inheritance is the Lord Himself, just as Aaron's was. The crux, the essence of our inheritance, is God in Christ—being in perfect fellowship with Him, without sin, dwelling in His presence, seeing Him face to face.

By the inspiration of the Spirit, Peter describes the nature of this inheritance:

Incorruptible/imperishable
It won't go bad or be suddenly lost, like an earthly inheritance can. Before the great stock market crash of 1929, many families had invested their inheritances in ways that they thought were secure; often their hope and security were in what was an unexpectedly perishable inheritance. It was suddenly taken away from them. My great-grandmother in the Netherlands was much the same: she owned rental real estate in the city of Rotterdam before World War II. War came; the German air force bombed much of the city, destroying her wealth and inheritance, leaving her a bitter and empty woman. Her heart had been set on life with an earthly inheritance that was destroyed. But God tells us here in His Word that we are born again to obtain an inheritance that is imperishable. It will not perish because it is kept by the Father.

Undefiled
Some earthly inheritances are gained and kept by sin; they are inherently corrupt and corrupting. But the inheritance of the children of the Father is a perfect inheritance. It is not stained by sin. It is good and holy because it is the treasure, the gift of the holy God, who is keeping it for us in a holy place.

Will not fade away
Just as it is imperishable, our inheritance as children of the Father will not fade away. It will not disappear slowly over time or through

eternity. We will not be able to use it up. Others will not be able to use it up. Sometimes on this earth, inheritances are eaten up by legal fees as families fight in court. Ours is not like that. As His children, we will enjoy the lavish riches of our heavenly Father forever—without ever diminishing them.

Reserved in heaven for you
Our inheritance is ready, it is waiting for us. It is at death, at the point of the completion of this earthly pilgrimage as a stranger in the world, that the believer comes home and enters into the fullness of the inheritance. We have glimmers and small foretastes of it on this earth, yet as 1 Corinthians 2:9 says, "Eye hath not seen, nor ear heard, neither have entered into the heart of man, the things which God hath prepared for them that love him"; it is ready and waiting, being kept by God for us, till the day of our appearing before Him.

The teaching of God's Word here in 1 Peter parallels that in the Old Testament. When God made the ancient Israelites His children—bringing them into covenant relation with Himself—He promised them an inheritance. For the nation of Israel, this inheritance was the promise of the land of Canaan: a fertile, beautiful land. In a tangible, immediate sense, Canaan was their God-given inheritance, though as Hebrews tells us, the faithful believers of Israel knew that even the inheritance of Canaan was only an earthly picture of a better reality to come. Even more than they looked to Canaan, they desired their heavenly inheritance in Christ (Hebrews 11).

In much the same way as the Old Testament saints, we enjoy earthly, tangible experiences, little tastes of our inheritance to come. For us in the New Testament era, these tastes are not in the land of Canaan or in the city of Jerusalem in Palestine, but in Christ's church, in communion with God in Christ and with His saints. Corporate worship, baptism, the Lord's Supper, and spiritual fellowship all foreshadow the fullness of our inheritance.

These are part of the Father's goodness to us as His children. They are encouragements, just as He encourages us in His Word. We, as children of the Father, are born again to receive a secure inheritance that is imperishable and undefiled, that will not fade away, and that is reserved in heaven for us. God is personal and direct in His Word.

Dear saints, dear children of the Father, this is reserved in heaven for *you*. This is what the Father has done for you, His amazing purpose, intent, and goal. But listen as our Lord speaks through His apostle even more.

What the Father Is Doing for You (1 Peter 1:5)

For those "who are kept by the power of God through faith unto salvation ready to be revealed in the last time" (1 Peter 1:5), the Father is doing something incredible.

We might think: "Well, the inheritance is secured by God, it is a secure inheritance, permanent, eternal—but what if I fail in the end to qualify for the inheritance? What if, through my sin, my failure, I am disqualified before God?" Or perhaps, as in the case of the believers here in our passage, scattered through Pontus, Galatia, Cappadocia, Asia, and Bithynia, "What if persecutions become so severe that I crack, that I fail, that I am unfaithful to Christ?"

Peter has already shown that God the Father is the one who has caused us to be born again through Jesus Christ. We are not saved because of our own actions or deeds, but by the grace of God alone. And here we see that our preservation and protection as children of the Father is also His work, the work of God! He will sustain His children, preserving them in faith in Christ through life and death, till they enter heavenly glory and their faith is made sight.

In the latter part of Romans 8, we see this same truth of the powerful protection of the children of the Father stated beautifully in another way: "[Nothing] shall be able to separate us from the love of God, which is in Christ Jesus our Lord" (v. 39). This verse is echoed in many of the summaries of biblical truth found in the creeds and confessions of Reformed and Presbyterian churches. The answer to Question 1 of the Heidelberg Catechism says, "[He] so preserves me that without the will of my heavenly Father, not a hair can fall from my head; yea, that all things must be subservient to my salvation." As the Westminster Confession of Faith puts it, "They, whom God has accepted in His Beloved, effectually called, and sanctified by His Spirit, can neither totally nor finally fall away from the state of grace, but shall certainly persevere therein to the end, and be eternally saved" (17:1). You see, as a child of the Father, you are kept and preserved by *His* power.

What is the most powerful thing you can think of? A fighter jet? a nuclear-powered aircraft carrier? a hurricane or earthquake? the sun, which heats our planet? These are created powers. Consider the creative and redemptive power of God! There is no greater power than God's—His power is infinite and eternal. Second Peter 3:7–13 says: "But the heavens and the earth, which are now, by the same word are kept in store, reserved unto fire against the day of judgment and perdition of ungodly men…in the which the heavens shall pass away with a great noise, and the elements shall melt with fervent heat, the earth also and the works that are therein shall be burned up…. Nevertheless we, according to his promise, look for new heavens and a new earth, wherein dwelleth righteousness." On that day, no one will be able to stand against the full display of God's power—and this is His power as Father that keeps His children!

Why Is the Father Doing This for You?
By His power, God is preserving the universe for that final day, just as by His power He is protecting and preserving us, His people, for that day, when the fullness of His salvation will be revealed: we are "kept by the power of God through faith unto salvation ready to be revealed in the last time" (1 Peter 1:5). Our heavenly Father is doing this for the full completion of our salvation—our resurrection, glorification, eternal security, the new heaven and earth, where we will dwell and delight forever in the presence of the Lord, in sweet communion with Father, Son, and Holy Spirit!

Brothers and sisters in the Lord, are you rejoicing and resting in the saving work of God in Jesus Christ? Do you love your heavenly Father? Are you filled with thankfulness as you consider your new life as a child of the Father, your secure and coming inheritance as a child of the Father, and your powerful protection as a child of the Father? Does your heart cry out: "Our Father which art in heaven, hallowed be Thy name. Thy kingdom come, Thy will be done, on earth as it is in heaven"?

Friends, if any of you are apart from Christ, not living by faith in Him, what you have read about is what the people of God have. They are children of the Father. And this is what the gospel of Jesus Christ calls and invites you to: to change from being an enemy of God and to become a child of God as your Father, because of and through the death and resurrection of His eternal Son. By God's grace, come to God in Christ so that you can join us with Peter and the church of all ages saying, "Blessed be the God and Father of our Lord Jesus Christ, which according to his abundant mercy hath begotten us again unto a lively hope...to an inheritance...kept by the power of God...unto salvation."

Brothers and sisters in Christ, being so secure, so blessed with an incredible inheritance, and brought back into relationship with the Father through the Son, given new life as children of God the Father, and all of this by the Father's great mercy—how then should we live? Like the apostle Peter, we should burst into worship and praise of God the Father, full of enthusiastic love and thankfulness. Let His praises overflow from your heart, from your lips: "Blessed be the God and Father of our Lord Jesus Christ!"

CHAPTER 5

Richard Sibbes on the Mercy and Faithfulness of the Father

Paul Smalley

Grace be to you and peace from God our Father, and from the Lord Jesus Christ. Blessed be God, even the Father of our Lord Jesus Christ, the Father of mercies, and the God of all comfort.... But as God is true, our word toward you was not yea and nay.

—2 Corinthians 1:2–3, 18

Richard Sibbes (1577–1635) was a powerful preacher known for his sweet and heavenly life.[1] His ministry spanned the first three and a half decades of the seventeenth century. He trained many Puritan ministers. After Sibbes died in 1635, Izaac Walton wrote:

---

1. For Sibbes's life and theology, see Mark E. Dever, *Richard Sibbes: Puritanism and Calvinism in Late Elizabethan and Early Stuart England* (Macon, Ga.: Mercer University Press, 2000); Sidney H. Rooy, "Richard Sibbes: The Theological Foundation of the Mission," in *The Theology of Missions in the Puritan Tradition: A Study of Representative Puritans: Richard Sibbes, Richard Baxter, John Eliot, Cotton Mather, and Jonathan Edwards* (Grand Rapids: Eerdmans, 1965), 15–65. For dissertations and theses related to Sibbes, see Frank E. Farrell, "Richard Sibbes: A Study in Early Seventeenth Century English Puritanism" (PhD diss., University of Edinburgh, 1955); Bert Affleck Jr., "The Theology of Richard Sibbes, 1577–1635" (PhD diss., Drew University, 1969); Harold P. Shelly, "Richard Sibbes: Early Stuart Preacher of Piety" (PhD diss., Temple University, 1972); Beth E. Tumbleson, "The Bride and Bridegroom in the Work of Richard Sibbes, English Puritan" (MA thesis, Trinity Evangelical Divinity School, 1984); Cary N. Weisiger, "The Doctrine of the Holy Spirit in the Preaching of Richard Sibbes" (PhD diss., Fuller Theological Seminary, 1984); Jonathan Jong-Chun Won, "Communion with Christ: An Exposition and Comparison of the Doctrine of Union and Communion with Christ in Calvin and the English Puritans" (PhD diss., Westminster Theological Seminary, 1989), 132–78; Stephen P. Beck, "The Doctrine of *Gratia Praeparans* in the Soteriology of Richard Sibbes" (PhD diss., Westminster Theological Seminary, 1994); Jean D. Williams, "The Puritan Quest for Enjoyment of God" (PhD diss., University of Melbourne, 1997).

Of this blest man, let this just praise be given,
Heaven was in him, before he was in heaven.[2]

His books were very popular. David Masson wrote, "From the year 1630, onwards for twenty years or so, no writings in practical theology seem to have been so much read among the pious English middle classes as those of Sibbes."[3] The seven volumes of Sibbes's collected works, edited in the nineteenth century by Alexander Grosart, have been reprinted and are available today.[4]

As we consider the beauty and glory of the heavenly Father, our aim here will be to listen to Sibbes on the subject of the mercy and faithfulness of the Father. Though I will draw from several treatises and sermons, our main source will be Sibbes's exposition of 2 Corinthians 1,[5] especially his exposition on verses 2–3 and 18, "Grace be to you and peace from God our Father, and from the Lord Jesus Christ. Blessed be God, even the Father of our Lord Jesus Christ, the Father of mercies, and the God of all comfort.... But as God is true, our word toward you was not yea and nay."

---

2. Cited in Stapleton Martin, *Izaak Walton and His Friends* (London: Chapman & Hall, 1903), 174.

3. David Masson, *The Life of John Milton* (Boston: Gould and Lincoln, 1859), 1:406.

4. *Works of Richard Sibbes*, ed. Alexander B. Grosart, 7 vols. (1862–1864; repr., Edinburgh: Banner of Truth, 2001). I will cite the *Works* alongside the seventeenth-century editions for easy reference. Dever remarks, "In the course of reading many of the sermons in the seventeenth-century texts, it became apparent that Grosart had been almost entirely accurate in his collected edition" (Dever, *Richard Sibbes*, 8).

5. Richard Sibbes, *Learned Commentary or Exposition upon the First Chapter of the Second Epistle of S. Paul to the Corinthians* (London: by J. L. for N. B., 1655). See *Works*, vol. 3. Other texts by Sibbes cited in this paper are *The Brvised Reede and Smoaking Flax* (London: for R. Dawlman, 1630); *The Christians Portion, or, The Charter of a Christian... Corrected and Enlarged* (London: by J. O. for John Rothwell, 1638); *An Exposition of the Third chapters of the Epistle of Saint Pavl to the Philippians* [etc.] (London: Peter Cole, 1647); *The Gloriovs Feast of the Gospel* (London: for John Rothwell, 1650); *A Heavenly Conference between Christ and Mary after His Resurrection* (London: John Rothwell, 1654); *Light from Heaven* (London: by E. Purslow for N. Bourne, 1638); *The Retvrning Backslider, or, A Commentarie upon the Whole XIII Chapter of the Prophecy of the Prophet Hosea* (London: by G. M. for George Edwards, 1639); *The Saints Cordials* (London: Robert Davvleman, 1629); *The Saints Safetie in Evill Times* (London: by M. Flesher for R. Dawlman, 1633); and "To the Reader," in Paul Baynes, *A Commentarie vpon the First Chapter of the Epistle of Saint Pavl, Written to the Ephesians* (London: by Thomas Snodham, for Robert Milbovrne, 1618).

I will organize Sibbes's teaching on divine mercy around three descriptions of God in the Scriptures: the Father of our Lord Jesus Christ, the Father of mercies, and the God who is true.

The Father of Our Lord Jesus Christ

We approach the Father through Christ in the Spirit.[6] The gospel is bound up in the doctrine of the Trinity. Paul Schaeffer writes that Sibbes's doctrine of salvation is "theocentric and trinitarian."[7] Sibbes said, "Our redemption is founded upon the joint agreement of all three persons of the Trinity."[8] God the Father is the fountain, God the Son is the conduit, and God the Spirit is the stream.[9] We must seek the Father through the Son, or we do not seek God at all.

God is the Father of Christ in a unique way. The risen Christ said to Mary Magdalene in John 20:17, "Go to my brethren, and say unto them, I ascend unto my Father, and your Father; and to my God, and your God." Christ distinguished between His sonship and our sonship: He said, "my Father and your Father," not "our Father." Sibbes explained: "God is Christ's Father from eternity.... Christ is co-equal with the Father in glory and majesty." The Father and the Son have one and the same essence. Sibbes said: "God is his Father in another manner than ours. He is his Father by nature, ours by adoption."[10]

He wrote: "He is the God and Father of Christ first, and then the Father of mercy, and the God of comfort. Take him out of this order, and think not of him as a God of comfort, but as a consuming fire."[11] He said: "He is holiness and purity.... We cannot endure the brightness of the majesty of the Father."[12]

---

6. On Sibbes's doctrine of the work of the Holy Spirit in believers, see Joel R. Beeke, "Richard Sibbes on Entertaining the Holy Spirit," in *The Beauty and Glory of the Holy Spirit*, ed. Joel R. Beeke and Joseph A. Pipa Jr. (Grand Rapids: Reformation Heritage Books, 2012), 227–45; Weisiger, "The Doctrine of the Holy Spirit in the Preaching of Richard Sibbes."

7. Paul R. Schaeffer Jr., *The Spiritual Brotherhood: Cambridge Puritans and the Nature of Christian Piety* (Grand Rapids: Reformation Heritage Books, 2011), 171.

8. Sibbes, *Brvised Reede and Smoaking Flax*, 7. See *Works*, 1:43.

9. Sibbes, *Learned Commentary* [on 2 Cor. 1], 43. See *Works*, 3:49. See also *Works*, 4:293.

10. Sibbes, *Heavenly Conference*, 112. See *Works*, 6:450.

11. Sibbes, *Learned Commentary* [on 2 Cor. 1], 43. See *Works*, 3:48.

12. Sibbes, *Christians Portion*, 153. See *Works*, 4:32.

The holy Father predestined His Son to be the Mediator and predestined His elect people to become sons by the incarnate Son's work, to the praise of His glorious grace.[13] Divine predestination binds us to Christ's humiliation and exaltation,[14] so that the Father who elected us in eternity past will be the Father who glorifies us unto eternity future.[15]

Our sin requires that we have a surety to pay our debts to God, or we shall pay them in hell. God is merciful, but He is also just. His anger burns against sin. That is not because God is evil: "He is good from himself, we provoke him to be severe."[16] God cannot show mercy at the expense of justice: "One attribute in God must not devour another; all must have satisfaction, his justice must have no wrong," Sibbes wrote. He said that God, "having punished our sins in our surety Christ," is now "our Father, he is the Father of mercies," and "his justice hath no loss by it."[17] This is crucial for us, for unless God's justice is satisfied and our sins are forgiven, all God's gifts to us are but "a feeding the traitor to the day of execution."[18]

Therefore, we must be joined to Jesus to call His Father our Father. Union with Christ is "the ground of all comfort."[19] All that is Christ's becomes ours. Christ's history becomes our history by our union with Him.[20] Sibbes explained that as our Mediator and Surety, all of Christ's work and all of God's blessing on Christ belong to the people united with Christ:

> Christ hath all first, and we have all from him: he is the first Son, and we are sons, he is the first beloved of God, and we

---

13. Sibbes, *Learned Commentary* [on 2 Cor. 1], 21. See *Works*, 3:27. Sibbes also affirmed the doctrine of reprobation (Dever, *Richard Sibbes*, 103–105). Regarding supralapsarianism and infralapsarianism, Dever comments, "Sibbes was decidedly agnostic in this discussion" (*Richard Sibbes*, 102). See Sibbes's summary of the positions and his remarks about our present limited knowledge in Sibbes, "To the Reader," in Baynes, *Commentarie*, A2r–3r. However, in at least one place Sibbes seemed to speak in infralapsarian terms, writing that God elected men as He saw them "defiled, lying in our filth" (*Works*, 1:9).

14. Sibbes, *Learned Commentary* [on 2 Cor. 1], 21. See *Works*, 3:27.

15. Sibbes, *Heavenly Conference*, 122. See *Works*, 6:453.

16. Sibbes, *Learned Commentary* [on 2 Cor. 1], 29. See *Works*, 3:35.

17. Sibbes, *Learned Commentary* [on 2 Cor. 1], 23. See *Works*, 3:28.

18. Sibbes, *Learned Commentary* [on 2 Cor. 1], 26. See *Works*, 3:31.

19. Sibbes, *Learned Commentary* [on 2 Cor. 1], 21. See *Works*, 3:27.

20. See Affleck, "The Theology of Richard Sibbes," 109.

are beloved in him; he is filled first with all grace, and we are filled from him, *of his fullness we receive grace for grace* [John 1:16]: he was first acquitted of our sins, as our surety, and then we are justified; because he was justified from our sins, being our surety, he is ascended into heaven, we shall ascend; he sits at the right hand of God, and we sit with him in heavenly places; he judgeth, we shall judge [with] him; whatsoever we do, Christ doth it first, we have it in Christ, and through Christ, and from Christ; he is the Father of Christ, and our Father.[21]

So by His grace, the Lord Jesus is able to include us in the marvelous words, "my Father, and your Father." Christ in "his infinite mercy" calls us "brethren," brothers and sisters under His Father. Sibbes said, "God is our Father by virtue of Christ's satisfaction to justice, and conquest over all our enemies."[22] He wrote, "He is beloved of the Father first; *in him I am well-pleased* [Matt. 3:17].... He delights in us, because we are one with Christ, in whom he beholds us."[23]

Therefore, by way of application, we must always approach the Father through Christ or we deny ourselves the peace of the gospel. Sibbes wrote: "God reconciled in Christ will pacify the conscience, nothing else will do it. For if our chief peace were fetched from sanctification (as many fetch it thence in error of judgment) alas the conscience would be dismayed, and always doubt whether it had sanctification enough or no." He said that sanctification is indeed a necessary "qualification" for us to have assurance. But it is not the "foundation of comfort."[24]

To rest in God's mercy, we must rest upon the gospel of Christ. Sibbes said, "When faith considers God pictured out in the gospel, it sees him the Father of Christ, and our Father, and the Father of mercies and God of comforts; faith seeing infinite mercy in an infinite God."[25] He wrote that there is "nothing more terrible" than thinking of God apart from Christ, but "nothing more sweet" than thinking of God in Christ.[26] Sibbes counseled:

---

21. Sibbes, *Learned Commentary* [on 2 Cor. 1], 21. See *Works*, 3:27. Cf. *Works*, 4:463; 6:460; 7:216.

22. Sibbes, *Heavenly Conference*, 112. See *Works*, 6:450.

23. Sibbes, *Christians Portion*, 157–58. See *Works*, 4:33.

24. Sibbes, *Learned Commentary* [on 2 Cor. 1], 15. See *Works*, 3:20–21.

25. Sibbes, *Learned Commentary* [on 2 Cor. 1], 32. See *Works*, 3:37.

26. Sibbes, *Christians Portion*, 164. See *Works*, 4:34.

Let us lay it up, to put it in practice in the time of dissolution [death], in the time of spiritual conflict, in the time when our consciences shall be awakened (and perhaps upon the rack), and Satan will be busy to trouble our peace; that we may shut our eyes to all things below, and see God shining on [us] in Christ; that we may see the favor of God in Christ, by whose death and passion he is reconciled to us, and in the grace and free favor of God in Christ we shall see peace enough.[27]

If God is merciful in Christ, then there is "a haven to flee to" from the wrath of God. Sibbes urged, "Therefore despair not thou drooping soul, whosoever thou art that art under the guilt of sin, come to the Father of mercies, cast thyself into this sea of his mercy." We ought not to say that our sins are too great. God has infinite mercy in His nature, and Christ has paid the price to make an infinite satisfaction to God's justice for sin. "There is mercy for thee if thou wilt come in."[28] "Thy sins are all as a spark of fire that falls into the ocean," where it disappears immediately.[29]

We must not dare to trample on God's mercy by twisting it into an excuse for sin.[30] God is not only the Father of mercy; He is the God of vengeance and justice, too.[31] When God is most feared the sinner is most ready for mercy. Sibbes said, "This oil of mercy it is put in broken vessels, it is kept best there, a broken heart, a humble heart, receives and keeps mercy."[32]

Yet when sinners loaded with guilt cry out for mercy, they can rest assured that God "is more willing to pardon than they are to ask mercy."[33] Like the father in the parable of the prodigal son, Sibbes said, "You shall find that God by his Spirit will be readier to meet you, than you are to cast yourselves at the feet of his mercy, and into the arms of his mercy: he will come and meet you, and kiss you."[34]

When God gives you "an excellent inward peace" in your heart and conscience, it will support you in all trials and sorrows with an

27. Sibbes, *Learned Commentary* [on 2 Cor. 1], 15. See *Works*, 3:21.
28. Sibbes, *Learned Commentary* [on 2 Cor. 1], 25. See *Works*, 3:31.
29. Sibbes, *Learned Commentary* [on 2 Cor. 1], 29. See *Works*, 3:35.
30. Sibbes, *Learned Commentary* [on 2 Cor. 1], 26. See *Works*, 3:32.
31. Sibbes, *Learned Commentary* [on 2 Cor. 1], 27. See *Works*, 3:32.
32. Sibbes, *Learned Commentary* [on 2 Cor. 1], 28. See *Works*, 3:34.
33. Sibbes, *Learned Commentary* [on 2 Cor. 1], 31. See *Works*, 3:36.
34. Sibbes, *Learned Commentary* [on 2 Cor. 1], 34. See *Works*, 3:40.

assurance of the Father's love and forgiveness. Nothing puts such a sting into "losses, crosses, banishment, imprisonment, and death" like a fearful and guilty conscience. But "make conscience good" by Christ, Sibbes said, and "Thou shalt hold up thy head…nothing shall daunt or appall thy courage."[35] In Christ, He is our Father. Sibbes wrote, "He can as soon cease to love his Son, as cease to love us."[36]

God is the Father of our Lord Jesus Christ.

The Father of Mercies

God is merciful by nature. Mercy is grace or free favor to a person in misery.[37] Misery is the magnet of mercy.[38] And God is full of mercy; it is His heart and soul—His very name (Ex. 34:6).[39] Sibbes said, "He that is great in majesty is abounding in mercy."[40] The sea is not more naturally flowing and wet, and the sun does not more naturally shine, than God naturally shows mercy.[41] Mercy "is his nature, it is himself."[42] "He delighteth in mercy" (Mic. 7:18).[43]

Sibbes wrote, "Mercy is God's sweetest attribute, which sweeteneth all his other attributes; for but for mercy, whatsoever else is in God, were matter of terror to us."[44] However, in Christ, Sibbes wrote, "He will be glorified in showing mercy."[45] "He doth all for the glory of his mercy, both in the creation, and in the gospel."[46]

God's love and mercy are major themes in the theology of Sibbes. Mark Dever writes that he portrayed Christianity as "the story of God's love," wherein the Father chooses sinners to be His people,

---

35. Sibbes, *Retvrning Backslider*, 120–21. See *Works*, 2:298.

36. Sibbes, *Heavenly Conference*, 149. See *Works*, 6:461.

37. Sibbes, *Learned Commentary* [on 2 Cor. 1], 24. See *Works*, 3:28. The definition of mercy vis-à-vis misery goes back to Cicero and Seneca, was picked up by Augustine, and carried on by Reformers such as Wolfgang Musculus (Richard Muller, *Post-Reformation Reformed Dogmatics* [Grand Rapids: Baker, 2004], 3:575).

38. "Misery being the loadstone of mercy" (Sibbes, *Learned Commentary* [on 2 Cor. 1], 37. See *Works*, 3:42). The link between misery and mercy is even clearer in their Latin equivalents: *miseria et misericordia*.

39. Sibbes, *Learned Commentary* [on 2 Cor. 1], 30. See *Works*, 3:35.

40. Sibbes, *Retvrning Backslider*, 106. See *Works*, 2:292.

41. Sibbes, *Learned Commentary* [on 2 Cor. 1], 21. See *Works*, 3:27.

42. Sibbes, *Learned Commentary* [on 2 Cor. 1], 23. See *Works*, 3:28.

43. Sibbes, *Learned Commentary* [on 2 Cor. 1], 30. See *Works*, 3:35.

44. Sibbes, *Retvrning Backslider*, 106. See *Works*, 2:292.

45. Sibbes, *Learned Commentary* [on 2 Cor. 1], 24. See *Works*, 3:29–30.

46. Sibbes, *Learned Commentary* [on 2 Cor. 1], 25. See *Works*, 3:31.

indeed, to be His "best friends."[47] This is the "principal favor" of the covenant of grace.[48]

God is not only merciful, but also the Father of mercies. Sibbes considered the word *Father* to sum up all the promises of the gospel.[49] Geoffrey Nuttall wrote, "Throughout Puritanism God's Fatherhood is a favourite and insistent theme."[50] Sibbes said, "There is a world of riches in this, to be the sons of God."[51]

God is the Father par excellence. Sibbes asked, "What may we expect from God, being a Father?" He answered: "We may expect whatsoever a child may expect from a father. God taketh not upon him empty names." He added, "The true reality of fatherhood is in God." Whatever kindnesses are in the heart of a father "we may expect from God our Father, and infinite more."[52] God looks upon the members of Christ with the same kind of "eternal sweet tenderness" He has for His Son.[53]

God shows Himself to be the Father of mercies in all His dealings with us. Before our conversion, He is the Father of mercies in "offering and enjoining [urging] mercy" to us in the gospel. In mercy, He patiently defers His wrath. When we are converted, He is the Father of mercies "in pardoning sin freely, in pardoning all sin, the punishment and the guilt, and all." When we are living under His grace, He is the Father of mercies "to correct his children seasonably," yet to soften and sweeten His correction with comforts. His mercies are new every day (Lam. 3:22–23).[54] He has the affection of a mother for her children,[55] and like a father accepts our obedience though it is "feeble and weak."[56] Everything that "comes from God to his children" is "dipped in mercy."[57]

47. Dever, *Richard Sibbes*, 106–107. He cites Sibbes, *Works*, 1:9; 2:73; 6:241; 5:516; 4:98; 2:216; 6:232, 235; 1:262.
48. Dever, *Richard Sibbes*, 114–15. He cites Sibbes, *Works*, 6:8, 20; 5:263; 2:253–54.
49. Sibbes, *Exposition* [Phil. 3, etc.], 2:97. See *Works*, 5:25.
50. Geoffrey F. Nuttall, *The Holy Spirit in Puritan Faith and Experience* (Oxford: Basil Blackwell, 1946), 63. See Joel R. Beeke, *Heirs with Christ: The Puritans on Adoption* (Grand Rapids: Reformation Heritage Books, 2008).
51. Sibbes, *Light from Heaven*, 2:20. See *Works*, 4:502.
52. Sibbes, *Heavenly Conference*, 114–115. See *Works*, 6:451.
53. Sibbes, *Heavenly Conference*, 149. See *Works*, 6:461.
54. Sibbes, *Learned Commentary* [on 2 Cor. 1], 24. See *Works*, 3:30.
55. Sibbes, *Learned Commentary* [on 2 Cor. 1], 30. See *Works*, 3:35.
56. Sibbes, *Learned Commentary* [on 2 Cor. 1], 56–57. See *Works*, 3:61.
57. Sibbes, *Learned Commentary* [on 2 Cor. 1], 25. See *Works*, 3:30.

How should Christians respond to the Father of mercies? First, believers should crave and pray for a deeper experiential knowledge of our Father's mercy for us. Like the apostle Paul, Sibbes desired that every Christian enjoy "this shining of God into the heart, this shedding [pouring out] of the love of God into the heart" in ever greater ways.[58] This, Sibbes wrote, "is a real comfort, inward and spiritual, by the assistance and strength of the Spirit of God, when perhaps there is no outward thing to comfort."[59] This knowledge does not come through a mystical vision, but by the gaze of faith on the Father's heart as He has revealed Himself in Christ. There are degrees of experience of the Spirit of adoption.[60] Let us long for more.

Nothing will transform us like an experiential knowledge of God's love for us in Jesus Christ. Sibbes wrote, "One glance of his fatherly countenance in Jesus Christ, will banish all terrors whatsoever, and make even a very dungeon to be a paradise."[61] When our hearts feel "cold, and dead," we must labor to embrace the Father's mercy by faith. His affection will warm in us "new love, and new affections to one another." Sibbes invites us, "Let us come to this light of God's love in Christ, and by oft meditation of God's Word, see there how he presents himself to us a Father in covenant; not only a friend, but a Father, a gracious Father."[62]

Second, the knowledge of the Father's mercies moves God's children to praise and worship Him. Sibbes wrote, "It is the disposition of God's children (after they have tasted the sweet mercy and comfort and love of God) to break forth into the praising of God and to thanksgiving." This is as natural for them as it is "for the birds to sing in the spring."[63] The "wonderful mercy" that the majestic God would adopt "traitors, rebels, enemies, to make them his sons"[64] inspires "a mixed affection of fear and love," for our Father is fearsome in His greatness and lovely in His goodness.[65]

---

58. Sibbes, *Learned Commentary* [on 2 Cor. 1], 11. See *Works*, 3:16.

59. Sibbes, *Learned Commentary* [on 2 Cor. 1], 39. See *Works*, 3:44.

60. Sibbes, *Heavenly Conference*, 142. See *Works*, 6:458. Cf. also *Works*, 5:26.

61. Sibbes, *Learned Commentary* [on 2 Cor. 1], 48. See *Works*, 3:53.

62. Sibbes, *The Saints Cordials*, 100. See *Works*, 6:398.

63. Sibbes, *Learned Commentary* [on 2 Cor. 1], 16. See *Works*, 3:22. Cf. also Sibbes, *Learned Commentary* [on 2 Cor. 1], 17. See *Works*, 3:23.

64. Sibbes, *Heavenly Conference*, 132. See *Works*, 6:456.

65. Sibbes, *Heavenly Conference*, 120. See *Works*, 6:452.

Third, the children of God must imitate our Father in showing mercy to others. If we do not bear the likeness of the Father of mercy, then we have no right to call Him our Father. If we are adopted by the Father, we have been ingrafted into the Son, and are becoming like Christ: patient, obedient, humble, "full of goodness, full of love."[66] He said, "This should stir us up to an imitation of this our gracious Father: for every father begets to his own likeness, and all the sons of this Father are like the Father, they are merciful." Luke 6:36 says, "Be ye therefore merciful, as your Father also is merciful." We must deal with people in need with "sweet mercy."[67]

The Father of mercies begets a spiritual family of mercy. Union with Christ makes us true Christians, but each Christian must be "a member of some particular congregation."[68] It is God's way to comfort His people by each Christian sharing his divine comforts with the others: "No man is for himself alone."[69] All Christians are brothers and sisters, and essentially equal.[70] Pride closes our hearts to the help we need from others so that we "bleed inwardly" but have no one to help.[71] Therefore, let God's beloved children humbly love each other (Col. 3:12).

Fourth, Christians can entrust their children into the hands of the Father of mercies. When standing up for Christ may cost us dearly, Christians ask, "What will become of my dear children if I do thus and thus?" Sibbes reminded us that God is a Father to the fatherless and a defender of widows (Ps. 68:5). He said that parents need to realize that God cares for their children: "We are but instruments, God is the chief Father, best and last Father."[72]

Fifth, God's mercies invite us to cry to Him even out of the depths of misery (Ps. 130:1). Sibbes wrote, "We have deep misery... yet notwithstanding, his mercy is deeper than our misery."[73] One reason why God allows His children to fall into great sorrows and distresses is so that He can show them that no matter how deep they

---

66. Sibbes, *Heavenly Conference*, 126–27. See *Works*, 6:454.
67. Sibbes, *Learned Commentary* [on 2 Cor. 1], 34–35. See *Works*, 3:40.
68. Sibbes, *Learned Commentary* [on 2 Cor. 1], 6. See *Works*, 3:11.
69. Sibbes, *Learned Commentary* [on 2 Cor. 1], 63. See *Works*, 3:67.
70. Sibbes, *Learned Commentary* [on 2 Cor. 1], 4. See *Works*, 3:10.
71. Sibbes, *Learned Commentary* [on 2 Cor. 1], 63. See *Works*, 3:68.
72. Sibbes, *Retvrning Backslider*, 114. See *Works*, 2:296.
73. Sibbes, *Learned Commentary* [on 2 Cor. 1], 31. See *Works*, 3:36.

go in misery, His mercy is deeper still.[74] In the end, God "will do like a tender-hearted mother, wiping away all tears from our eyes."[75]

Let us pray with confidence that our Father will meet our needs, both temporal and eternal.[76] Christ said in Luke 12:32, "Fear not, little flock; for it is your Father's good pleasure to give you the kingdom." Sibbes wrote, "He that will give you a kingdom, will not he give you daily bread?"[77] Let us pray expecting good gifts. Sibbes said, "Either we shall have what we want and lack, or else we shall have that which is better; he is a wise Father."[78] He wrote:

> And when all is taken from us in losses and crosses, to think, Well; our fathers may die, and our mothers may die, and our nearest, and dearest friends...may die; but we have a Father of mercy, that hath eternal mercy in him, his mercies are tender mercies, and everlasting mercies, as himself is.... When all are taken away, God takes not himself away, he is the Father of mercy still.[79]

The God and Father of our Lord Jesus Christ is the Father of mercies. But how does the sinner know that this is true? How can he be sure when conscience burns? This brings us to consider the third description of the Father that Sibbes gives us.

The God Who Is True

Paul wrote in 2 Corinthians 1:18, "But as God is true, our word toward you was not yea and nay." Sibbes said that if He is God, He must also be "unchangeable, eternal, immutable, almighty, all-sufficient...the author of all good in the creature." If He were otherwise, He would not be God.[80] Sibbes said: "God is faithful...in his nature. He is I Am, always like himself, immutable and unchangeable."[81]

God's truth colors all His ways with perfect truthfulness. Sibbes wrote: "God is true in his nature, and true in his free promises, and

74. Sibbes, *Retvrning Backslider*, 108–109. See *Works*, 2:293.

75. Sibbes, *Gloriovs Feast of the Gospel*, 79. See *Works*, 2:482.

76. Sibbes, *Heavenly Conference*, 123. See *Works*, 6:453.

77. Sibbes, *Heavenly Conference*, 118. See *Works*, 6:452.

78. Sibbes, *Heavenly Conference*, 121. See *Works*, 6:453.

79. Sibbes, *Learned Commentary* [on 2 Cor. 1], 36. See *Works*, 3:42.

80. Sibbes, *Learned Commentary* [on 2 Cor. 1], 379. See *Works*, 3:361.

81. Sibbes, *The Saints Safetie in Evill Times*, 2:170–71. See *Works*, 1:411. This paragraph is an example of Sibbes's use of scholastic terminology in the doctrine of God.

threatenings; he is true in his works, true in his Word, every way true. He is true in his nature, all is true within him.... God is true in all his purposes, true in his free and voluntary decrees. It was free for him to decree, but having decreed, there is a necessity of performing it; it is of the necessity of his nature as he is God."[82]

Sibbes established his worldview upon this basic reality: "It is the prime truth of all truths, that God is, and God is true.... It is a fundamental thing."[83] Sibbes wrote, "God is faithful...in his Word; he expresseth himself as he is; the Word that comes from God is an expression of the faithfulness of his nature."[84]

Sibbes taught the inerrancy of Scripture based on the truthfulness of God. The Scriptures are "most certain, even as certain as God himself." The Bible is "truth without error: authentical without appeal." It is "infallibly true without danger of error." It has supreme authority in everything it reveals. "There is nothing higher but God himself, whose Word it is; and it hath the same authority that himself hath." Church councils, traditions, and popes contradict each other; Scripture alone is the divine judge of all religious controversies because "Scripture" is "the Voice, and Word of God."[85]

God's faithfulness in His Word is also reflected in His faithfulness in His actions. Sibbes wrote, "God is faithful...in his works; Thou art good, and doest good, as the psalmist saith [Ps. 119:68]."[86] God is faithful in all His "relations." He is faithful as Creator, upholding His creations, giving them life, being, and motion as long as He wills for them to continue. He is faithful as Lord, and we must not argue with Him about why He makes one rich and another poor. He is faithful as Judge to reward everyone according to his works, punishing sin sometimes inwardly in the conscience and sometimes outwardly, and rewarding those faithful to Him.[87]

Best of all, "he is a true Father," faithful to His children. He corrects them when it is best. He rewards and encourages them when it is best. He will give an inheritance to His children. He has compassion on His children. Human fathers may act out of the whim of

82. Sibbes, *Learned Commentary* [on 2 Cor. 1], 379. See *Works*, 3:360–61.
83. Sibbes, *Learned Commentary* [on 2 Cor. 1], 380. See *Works*, 3:362.
84. Sibbes, *The Saints Safetie in Evill Times*, 2:171. See *Works*, 1:411.
85. Sibbes, *Learned Commentary* [on 2 Cor. 1], 385. See *Works*, 3:364–65.
86. Sibbes, *The Saints Safetie in Evill Times*, 2:171. See *Works*, 1:411.
87. Sibbes, *Learned Commentary* [on 2 Cor. 1], 381. See *Works*, 3:362.

strong emotions, but the divine Father acts out of truth and good-ness.[88] Sibbes said, "Therefore ever when thou art disappointed with men, retire to God and to his promises."[89]

God's truthfulness has direct bearing on the application of His mercy. We should gather God's promises and never let them go. If God is faithful, then His promises are worth more than gold. Sibbes wrote: "Treasure up all the promises we can, of the forgiveness of sins, of protection and preservation, that he will never leave us, but be our God to death, etc. and then consider withal, that he is faithful in performing the same.... In all the unfaithfulness of men whom thou trusteth, depend upon this, that God is still the same, and will not deceive thee."[90]

Find solid comfort by resting on God's Word. Our comfort in God's mercy depends on the degree to which we believe that God is true. Sibbes exhorted us "not to think God's Word to be too good to be true, but yield obedience to it: yield the obedience of faith to it in the promises. Here is a foundation for faith." Sibbes said, "Rely on the Word: wrestle with him when his dealings seem contrary; though his dealings with us seem to be yea, and nay.... Therefore let us not forsake our own mercy. This will uphold us, as in all tempta-tions, so in divine temptations, when God seems to forsake us: so Christ himself our blessed head did."[91]

Above all and in all, exercise faith in the Father through Jesus Christ. Sibbes said: "Beloved, live upon this.... Here is the love of God the Father, who is content to be a Father even in our sinful con-dition. If God be a Father to us, as to Christ, then let not our hearts be discouraged, in affliction, persecutions, temptations."[92]

Beloved, live upon this!

---

88. Sibbes, *Learned Commentary* [on 2 Cor. 1], 381. See *Works*, 3:363.
89. Sibbes, *The Saints Safetie in Evill Times*, 2:176. See *Works*, 1:412.
90. Sibbes, *The Saints Safetie in Evill Times*, 2:173–74. See *Works*, 1:412.
91. Sibbes, *Learned Commentary* [on 2 Cor. 1], 387. See *Works*, 3:368–69.
92. Sibbes, *Heavenly Conference*, 135–36. See *Works*, 6:457.

KNOWING
GOD THE
FATHER
AS SAVIOR

CHAPTER 6

Seeing the Father in the Face of Jesus

Derek W. H. Thomas

Lord, we know not whither thou goest; and how can we know the way?... Shew us the Father, and it sufficeth us.

—John 14:5, 8

Following the death of King Edward VI in 1553, his sister Mary, a Roman Catholic, became queen of England. A priest discovered a young man, William Hunter, reading the Bible in English, and he was arrested. For the next twenty months, he was urged to recant or face execution. Despite torture and unimaginable brutalization, he refused to recant. On March 26, 1555, he was taken to Brentwood, where his brother recorded a conversation between the nineteen-year-old William and his father. Responding to the pleas of his father, William cited the words of Jesus in John 14:1, "Let not your heart be troubled." He continued, "God be with you, good father, and be of good comfort, when we shall all meet again and be merry." Chains were wrapped around him. His father urged him to think on the passion of Christ. Just before he died, William said to his father, "I am not afraid." Then, like Stephen in the book of Acts, he cried out, "Lord, receive my spirit."[1]

There is a sense in which the words of John 14:1–3 are "holy ground." Do you sometimes feel, when you read Scripture, that there are places that are especially "holy," and that you need to take the shoes off your feet to walk in these paths? Of course, all Scripture is God's Word (2 Tim. 3:16–17; 2 Peter 1:20–21), but there are some passages of Scripture that seem to say, "This is holy ground." For many

---

1. John Foxe, *Voices of the Martyrs* (Alachua, Fla.: Bridge-Logos, 2007), 155–56.

of us, the so-called "High Priestly Prayer" of Jesus, recorded in John 17, is just such a place. It is fascinating to me that we actually have John 17, because John must have been eavesdropping on this somewhat private conversation between Jesus and His heavenly Father. In the first fourteen verses of this chapter, Jesus refers to His Father twelve times. John did not have a recorder or notebook. Of course, the Holy Spirit enabled him to recall Jesus' words, but he must have been deeply impressed as he listened to these words and then wrote them down later for his Gospel.

John 14, 15, and 16 particularly, and also 17, give us the last words of Jesus on the eve of His crucifixion. What does Jesus want the church to know after He is gone? What, especially, do the disciples need to know when He will no longer be there, when physically He will be gone from their midst? He will no longer teach them or instruct them in the manner to which they had grown accustomed, or perform the works and miracles that He had performed in their presence. When He is returned to His Father, what do these disciples need to know?

The Trinity

Isn't it fascinating that the answer to that question is *the doctrine of the Trinity*? What Jesus teaches the disciples on the last evening of His earthly life is the contours of how the Father, Son, and Holy Spirit are all engaged in what theologians have expressed as the external operations of redemption (*opera ad extra trinitatis indivisa sum*). He does not explain Trinitarian involvement in redemption in the form that the great creeds of the early church pronounced that doctrine. He does not give it in the shape of the Nicene or the Constantinopolitan Creed of AD 325 and 385. He does not give it as the Westminster Confession, the 1689 Baptist Confession, or the Savoy Declaration express it. But if we analyze John 14, 15, and 16, we have the doctrine of the Trinity. Jesus says things such as, "I and my Father are one," and, "If I go away I will come to you again; I will send another Comforter, another Paraclete to you." In particular, Jesus says that the Holy Spirit, the representative agent of Christ, will come and continue the ministry of the (now) exalted Jesus. In effect, Jesus is talking about the doctrine of the Trinity, explaining it in personal and practical terms.

It is fascinating that the doctrine of the Trinity is not some recondite truth that we teach seminary students on a certain day of the year and then forget forever. The doctrine of the Trinity is an *essential* truth. It is Christianity 101. It often occurs to me that we should do a little surprise quiz in church every now and then: hand everyone a sheet of paper and a pen, and say, "You have three minutes; write down everything you know about the doctrine of the Trinity, without committing a major heresy." Answers might include, there is only *one* God, but there is *more than* One who is that one God because God the Father is God, God the Son is God, and God the Holy Spirit is God; and yet there is only one God. The results would be fascinating and perhaps disappointing.

What is going on at the start of this Upper Room Discourse? Jesus is saying to His disciples: "Let Me comfort you. Let Me bring you a word of assurance, a word that will go deep down into your souls and will be the very fiber of strength and vitality that enables you to face the coming days and weeks before the Holy Spirit comes. Dark times are ahead for Me and for you, and you will need supernatural strength to face it, as will I. Let Me talk to you about the Trinity."

The Father

Recently, I was reading the very large volume titled *A History of the American People* by Paul Johnson, a conservative, secular historian who has written some important things as a social commentator on our times. I thought I should read such a history since I live in the United States! There was something in it that astounded me. While writing about George Washington, Johnson gives the passing comment that there are 17,000 extant letters and papers of George Washington, but his father is only mentioned in two of them.[2] Apparently, Washington's day-to-day consciousness and awareness of his relationship to his earthly father was almost non-existent.

That could never, ever have been said of our Lord Jesus. He was always conscious of His heavenly Father, every day, every moment, from the time He was a little infant in the arms of Mary. Mary, and presumably Joseph, instructed Him and reminded Him of who He was. As Jesus began to read and assimilate information, memorizing

---

2. Paul Johnson, *A History of the American People* (New York: HarperCollins, 1998), 122.

portions of the Old Testament Scriptures; as He went into the syna-gogue in Nazareth, and later journeyed down to Jerusalem for feast days; as He began to assimilate a clear apprehension of His iden-tity as to who He actually was, and His mother told Him about the extraordinary way He was conceived and born, He developed a deep-rooted, immensely personal relationship with His heavenly Father. And here, in this closing passage on the eve of His betrayal and crucifixion, it is His heavenly Father to whom He speaks.

There are two things I want us to see, two questions that arise from the disciples. It looks as though these disciples are constantly interrupting Him. As a teacher, I feel that, when students are con-stantly interrupting and asking questions, sometimes you have to say: "Enough already; let me finish my thought. There will be time for questions later." But it looks as though in the upper room the disciples are constantly asking questions, and Jesus is wonderfully patient. Thomas interjects, then Philip; in just six or seven verses, two disciples interrupt Him. We would think they would sit there silently, taking it all in, assimilating every word, but they are full of questions. They do not understand what is happening. And they are afraid. Even though they have spent three extraordinary years in Jesus' presence in His school of theology, they are still ignorant of many things, espe-cially the reasons why Jesus is now talking about His death.

They ask two questions, and then each of them has a consequence that follows. So I have two principal points and two consequences.

Question #1: How Can We Know the Way to the Father?
First, Jesus says to the disciples and to Thomas in particular, "Do you not see that I am the only way to the Father?" That is the first thing He wants to teach them.

Thomas has interrupted Him in verse 5: "Lord, we know not whither thou goest; and how can we know the way?" Jesus has already told them that He *must* go to Jerusalem, where He will be betrayed, handed over to the scribes and Pharisees, and crucified (Matt. 16:21). That was in Caesarea Philippi. Jesus made it very clear that His journey lay in the direction of Jerusalem, that He had come to be the Messiah, the Savior, and that He would lay down His life on behalf of sinners. But Thomas doesn't get it. Sometimes Thomas is seen as a realist. Actually, I don't think he is a realist at all, but a pessimist. He is gloomy. His temperament is melancholy. His glass is always half empty.

I have a framed picture of Eeyore the donkey, A. A. Milne's adorable but somewhat gloomy character in *Winnie-the-Pooh*, that my daughter gave to me when she was about twelve. She was summing up her father. In the scene, Eeyore is saying, "Have a nice day, if it is a nice day, which I doubt." That is Thomas! He has a propensity to doubt, to lack faith. It is why we call him "Doubting Thomas." Later, Jesus would urge him to put his finger into His resurrected side, still bearing the marks of the spear wound (John 20:26–28). Out of these doubts, this melancholy, Thomas says, "Jesus, Thou art telling us that Thou art going to the Father, and how can we follow Thee there since *we* don't know the way, and how can we know the way?" That is Thomas's problem: he doesn't know the way to the Father. And Jesus says, "I am the way, the truth, and the life: no man cometh unto the Father, but by me" (14:6).

Jesus is the way to the Father. To be saved, you need a loving relationship with the Father. Salvation is first of all a relationship with God in which we are His children and He is our heavenly Father. By nature we are "children of wrath" (Eph. 2:3). By grace through faith alone in Christ alone, we become children of the heavenly Father— adopted sons who may call upon God as "Abba, Father" (Rom. 8:15; Gal. 4:6). The logic of salvation in the Scriptures is that we come to the Father through the mediation of the Son and by the help of the Holy Spirit. It is always that way. Jesus is saying to Thomas: "You come to the Father. That is the most important thing—a relationship with a heavenly Father." So when the disciples come to Him, asking, "Teach us to pray," He says, "Our Father which art in heaven, Hallowed be thy name. Thy kingdom come. Thy will be done in earth, as it is in heaven.… For thine is the kingdom, and the power, and the glory, for ever. Amen" (Matt. 6:9–13).

Christians often ask, "Why is Jesus not mentioned in the Lord's Prayer?" That question reveals a fundamental misunderstanding of the nature of the way in which the gospel works in the New Testament. It brings us into a relationship with a heavenly Father. The self-awareness and self-consciousness that Jesus has in His incarnate state is a relationship with a heavenly Father. "I am the way to the Father, and I am the truth in the sense that He is true, as the Old

Testament was just a shadow," Jesus is saying. "If you want to know true life, then it is in relationship with God our heavenly Father, and you come to know that life, and that truth, and that way *by Me.*"

Do *you* have a saving relationship with the Father in heaven? Are you conscious of being His son, adopted into a family in which Jesus is your Elder Brother?

The First Consequence: Exclusivity

Jesus' statement about being the *only* way to the Father is very exclusive. Jesus allows no room for others—no other religion or Savior but Himself. Such exclusivity was immediately understood by the disciples at Pentecost; Peter, under threat of persecution, insisted, "Neither is there salvation in any other; for there is none other name under heaven given among men, whereby we must be saved" (Acts 4:12).

We live in an age of pluralism and relativism. Our postmodern world is suspicious of exclusive statements (except ones that state that exclusivity is wrong!). There is no such thing as "true truth"— the mantra of our times is "What is true for you isn't necessarily true for me." But here in John 14, Jesus is saying something that is absolutely exclusive: "You cannot come to an assurance of salvation unless you come through Me, and Me alone." If we say, "There is no other Mediator between God and man but Jesus Christ—not Hinduism, not Islam, not Buddhism, not Shintoism, not tree-hugging, nothing," it comes across in the world today as bigotry and hate-speech. If someone says, "No one has all the truth except me," it comes across in our postmodern world as judgmental and unloving. To cite D. A. Carson:

> Intolerance is no longer a refusal to allow contrary opinions to say their piece in public, but must be understood to be any questioning or contradicting the view that all opinions are equal in value, that all worldviews have equal worth, that all stances are equally valid. To question such postmodern axioms is by definition intolerant.[3]

But Jesus is saying, "Unless you have a relationship with Jesus Christ as Lord and Savior, you cannot be saved, you cannot be a Christian, and you cannot know God in a saving way." To be a

---

3. D. A. Carson, *The Intolerance of Tolerance* (Grand Rapids: Eerdmans, 2012), 11–12.

follower of Christ is to be a follower of One who claimed exclusivity. It was all or nothing. He did not share this with others. He alone is the way to God. In the words of Thomas à Kempis in his famous book, *The Imitation of Christ*: "Without the way there is no going. Without the truth there is no knowing. Without the life there is no living."[4]

Question #2: Can You Show Us the Father?

Philip speaks up, and he, too, has a question: "Jesus, is it possible for Thee to give us a little glimpse of the Father?" He says, "Shew us the Father, and it sufficeth us" (John 14:8). If only Jesus would do for the disciples what Moses did and reveal something of the glory of the Father.

Jesus appears to be disappointed when He responds to Philip. As incarnate Savior, Jesus demonstrated human affections and limitations without ever compromising His impeccability. He was tempted in every point as we are, yet without sin (Heb. 4:15). Jesus is disappointed with His disciples because they should know better. He has taught them and been with them for three years, yet they seem to understand so little. He says, as it were, "Have you been with Me for such a long time, and still you don't get it?" (cf. John 14:9). In truth, had they really understood who Jesus was, they would have understood that He *exegeted* for them the Father in heaven: "No man hath seen God at any time; the only begotten Son, which is in the bosom of the Father, he hath declared him" (1:18).[5] "Philip, if you had known Me," Jesus says in effect, "you would have seen something of what the Father is like, and through Me you would come to know Him" (cf. 14:7). Then He adds, "Believe me that I am in the Father, and the Father in me" (v. 11).

The statement Jesus makes in verse 11 is easily translated from the Greek. One could study Greek for three or four hours and be able to translate this verse into English: "I am in the Father, and the Father is in me." The use of small prepositions here is similar to their use in the Prologue to John's Gospel: "In the beginning was the Word...and the Word was God. The same was in the beginning with God" (1:1–2). In the beginning was the Word, "and the Word

---

4. Thomas à Kempis, *The Imitation of Christ* (Milwaukee, Wis.: Bruce Publishing Co., 1940), 108.

5. The Greek for "made him known" is ἐξηγήσατο, meaning "exegete."

was made flesh, and dwelt among us" (v. 14). It is very simple Greek. In the beginning, before creation, before there was anything, there was God. He exists already. And there was God *with* God—*God with God, and only one God.*

Your mind begins to ache as you try to ponder how there is only one God and yet there is plurality, fellowship *within* God (what the church fathers called, in Greek, *perichoresis*, or, in Latin, *circumincessio*). On the eve of His crucifixion, our Lord is thinking about His eternal relationship to the Father. He is *in* the Father and the Father is *in* Him. Philip says, "Shew us the Father," and Jesus responds, "Don't you understand that I am in the Father, and the Father is in Me?"

There is distinctiveness, there is separation, there is the Father and there is Jesus, they are separate identities and separate persons. One is the Father, the other is the Son, and yet Jesus is saying, "The Father is in me, and I am in the Father." The Father is not the Son; the Son is not the Father; the Father is not the Holy Spirit; the Holy Spirit is not the Father; the Holy Spirit is not the Son; the Son is not the Holy Spirit. There are these three, and they are *in* each other. They are not only *beside* each other (John 1:1) but *inside* each other. They are in communion, in fellowship with each other. The only thing that even remotely comes close to it in human terms is the relationship of marriage, when partners know each other so well they are inside each other's thoughts.

The Second Consequence: The Father Is Christlike

Augustine was asked, "What was God doing before He created the world?" We all know the sophistry of an upstart who thinks he has confounded you with the $64,000 question. Augustine answered, "Making hell for people who ask questions like that."[6] What a great answer given the sheer stupidity of the question! God was in love with Himself, and this love was not egotistic in any shape or form, because there is more than one who is the one God. There is plurality within the Godhead. God was going out toward Himself. He was in conversation, in fellowship, and in love. The Father was in love with His Son; the Son was in love with His Father. The Spirit

6. Augustine, *Confessions*, Chapter XI:10, "What God did Before the Creation of the World," *Nicene and Post-Nicene Fathers*, First Series, ed. Philip Schaff (Peabody, Mass.: Hendrickson, 2004), 1:167.

was in love with the Father and the Son. "I am in the Father, and the Father is in me."

When children ask you the great question, "What is God like?" do you feel as though you need a three-year course in systematic theology to answer it? The simplest Christian can answer that question: *He is like Jesus.* There is no un-Christlikeness in God. There is no un-Jesuslikeness in God. Jesus exegetes the Father; He tells us what the Father is like. That is why we read, "His name shall be called Wonderful, Counsellor, The mighty God, The everlasting Father, The Prince of Peace" (Isa. 9:6). Jesus is called "The everlasting Father" because the Father is like Jesus, and Jesus is like the Father. He shows us what the Father's heart is like. The gospel is not Jesus trying to win from the Father a love that He is reluctant to give. It is a travesty to view the gospel in that way. The Father's love is demonstrated in the gospel because He *gives* His only Son for us (John 3:16; Rom. 8:32).

Jesus goes on to explain to Philip how it is that He reveals the Father. He tells Philip that His words and works are not His own, but the Father's: "The words that I speak unto you I speak not of myself: but the Father that dwelleth in me, he doeth the works. Believe me that I am in the Father, and the Father in me: or else believe me for the very works' sake" (John 14:10–11). In John 5:17–19, Jesus explained what He meant by this:

> Jesus answered them, My Father worketh hitherto, and I work. Therefore the Jews sought the more to kill him.... Then answered Jesus and said unto them, Verily, verily, I say unto you, The Son can do nothing of himself, but what he seeth the Father do: for what things soever he doeth, these also doeth the Son likewise.

Jesus is giving a description of His relationship with the Father. Perhaps, from His incarnate point of view, He is drawing from His relationship with Joseph. Sometimes we downplay the influence of Joseph in Jesus' life because he goes into the background and presumably dies when Jesus is a teenager. But we can imagine here that Jesus is drawing from that earthly relationship. He would be in the carpenter shop and would pick up a piece of wood, saying to Joseph: "What is this piece of wood? What can we do with it?" Joseph would pick Him up and say, "Let me show you," and he would put an implement into His hand, put his own hand around his Son's hand, guide Him and direct Him. And Jesus' relationship with His heavenly Father was like that.

Remember the prophecy in Isaiah 50, where, in one of the Servant Songs, the prophet talks about looking forward to the coming of Jesus? Isaiah is given this insight: "The Lord God has given me the tongue of the learned" (Isa. 50:4). Jesus must have pondered these songs a great deal. He is taught by His heavenly Father. One imagines our Lord waking in the morning and asking, "What is my Father teaching Me today?"

What were the miracles but demonstrations of His Father's power? These miracles were displays of the Holy Spirit in the life of the Father's Son. The nature miracles of healing and restoration were, as it were, Jesus saying: "My heavenly Father wants to restore this broken world and bring it back to the Eden and the Paradise that it was meant to be. That is My Father's heart. Let Me show you what My Father is like." These miracles were demonstrations of what future reconstruction will look like. They are signals of the Father's intention for the fallen creation. That is what Jesus is doing in the Gospels—giving us a little foretaste of what the Father proposes when He creates the new heaven and new earth.

Then Jesus says, "Whatsoever ye shall ask in my name, that will I do, that the Father may be glorified in the Son" (John 14:13). Of course, here He is saying something about prayer. He is not saying that we can ask for anything, such as a fancy car, and God will give it to us. Of course not. The closer we walk with Jesus and with the heavenly Father, the more accurately our prayers will reflect what our Father wants us to ask. Actually, our prayers are fixed on the way up. As we send them, the Holy Spirit corrects them so that what the Father actually hears are the prayers we would have asked if we had known better and understood better. And those prayers are always answered.

Notice that in verse 13 we read, "that the Father may be glorified in the Son." Jesus not only shows the Father's words and the Father's works, but He also shows the Father's glory.

Concluding Applications
It is possible to miss the consequence of what Jesus is saying, just as Thomas and Philip did. We can be in the environment of Jesus and

fail to appreciate who Christ is and how He reveals the transcendent glory of His heavenly Father.

Have you been so long with Jesus that you have missed your heavenly Father? Maybe your relationship with your earthly father has thrown you for a loop, and you have all kinds of psychological consequences from that. Some associate their earthly families with emotional distress. They feel unloved or uncared-for in a way that makes it difficult to understand why talk of a heavenly Father should encourage us.

It is vitally important for us to appreciate that the gospel can break these negative feelings and replace them with something wonderful. In the gospel, you are introduced, through faith in Jesus, to a loving and gracious heavenly Father. Jesus comes to the vilest sinner, with His arms wide open, saying: "Come unto me, all ye that labour and are heavy laden, and I will give you rest. Take my yoke upon you, and learn of me; for I am meek and lowly in heart: and ye shall find rest unto your souls. For my yoke is easy, and my burden is light" (Matt. 11:28–29). Jesus says to you, "Let Me introduce you to My heavenly Father," and opening the door, He presents you to a gracious, loving heavenly Father who delights to give good things to His children.

When we come to our heavenly Father in this way, washed, forgiven, and adopted, we hear these words that are meant to reassure us: "Let not your heart be troubled" (John 14:1). Being a Christian does not exclude us from trials and difficulties. Indeed, the reverse is the case. Paul learned that, "we must through much tribulation enter into the kingdom of God" (Acts 14:22). Jesus knows all about trouble. Of course He does; He speaks these words to His disciples on the eve of His crucifixion. You may be in the darkest possible place, but He is telling you not to be afraid.

Have you ever been in a cave where there is no ambient light and you cannot even see your hand in front of you? It is absolutely pitch dark. It is quite an experience. It is daunting because you cannot see anything whatsoever. But right in front of you, if only you would reach out and touch Him, is your Savior with His arms outstretched to help you.

Do not be dismayed; let not your hearts be troubled. Don't be fearful or fretful. When somebody comes behind you and says,

"Boo!" you don't have to jump, you don't have to be afraid. When bad news arrives, a doctor's phone call, a test report in the mail, a call from your boss, whatever it is, you may rest in the assurance that Jesus will lead you, guide you, and protect you, no matter how dark it may be.

If you are in union and communion with our Lord Jesus Christ, ultimately, everything will be fine. You may lose your home, you may lose your job, you may lose your health, or Jesus may take you home to be with Him. But, "In my Father's house are many mansions" (John 14:2). Actually, that is a translation from the Latin *Vulgate*. We like to think we are going to a mansion, but perhaps a dwelling place is the idea here. The idea is "home." That's what heaven is, a place we will immediately think of as "home."

Isn't it wonderful to know that you are Christian and that these promises and reassurances are yours? Are *you* a Christian?

CHAPTER 7

The Apostle John and the Puritans on the Father's Adopting, Transforming Love

Joel R. Beeke

> *Behold, what manner of love the Father hath bestowed upon us, that we should be called the sons of God: therefore the world knoweth us not, because it knew him not. Beloved, now are we the sons of God, and it doth not yet appear what we shall be: but we know that, when he shall appear, we shall be like him; for we shall see him as he is. And every man that hath this hope in him purifieth himself, even as he is pure.*
>
> —1 John 3:1–3[1]

Several years ago, I was given an assignment to write a chapter for a book on how the Puritans viewed the believer's spiritual adoption into God's family. I felt some angst when I came across the observation of J. I. Packer, who said, "The Puritan teaching on the Christian life, so strong in other ways, was notably deficient" on adoption.[2] My angst increased when I read Erroll Hulse's assertion that "the Puritans did little in exploring this truth apart from a few paragraphs here and there."[3] Statements such as these promote the common opinion that adoption is *the* neglected aspect in the Puritan presentation of the *ordo salutis* ("plan of salvation"). So how could I write a whole chapter on the Puritan view of adoption when, as these men said, the Puritans wrote little or nothing of substance on the subject?

---

1. Portions of this chapter are adapted from my *The Epistles of John* (Darlington, U.K.: Evangelical Press, 2006), 111–20, and my *Heirs with Christ: The Puritans on Adoption* (Grand Rapids: Reformation Heritage Books, 2008), 75–102.

2. J. I. Packer, *Knowing God* (Downers Grove, Ill.: InterVarsity, 1973), 207.

3. Erroll Hulse, "Recovering the Doctrine of Adoption," *Reformation Today* 105 (1988): 10.

But then I remembered that Chapter XII of the Westminster Confession of Faith is the first confessional statement ever composed on adoption, and it was composed by Puritans. As I went from the confession to various old Puritan tomes, my fears dissipated. Soon, I realized that I had discovered a gold mine of thousands of pages of material the Puritans had written on adoption, and that no one had written anything significant on this subject in all the massive corpus of secondary Puritan literature.

The evidence suggests that adoption, though not developed as thoroughly as doctrines such as justification, sanctification, and assurance, was certainly not a neglected topic among the Puritans. William Ames, Thomas Watson, Samuel Willard, and Herman Witsius gave it ample treatment in their systematic theologies—Witsius devoting twenty-eight pages to it in his landmark work *The Economy of the Covenants between God & Man.*[4]

William Perkins, often called the father of Puritanism, addresses various aspects of adoption at some length in at least nine places in his works.[5] William Bates, Hugh Binning, Thomas Brooks, Anthony Burgess, Stephen Charnock, George Downame, John Flavel, Thomas Goodwin, William Gouge, Ezekiel Hopkins, Edward Leigh, and John Owen all provide some treatment of the subject.[6] Other Puritans, such

---

4. William Ames, *The Marrow of Theology,* trans. and ed. John D. Eusden (Boston: Pilgrim Press, 1968), 164–67; Thomas Watson, *A Body of Divinity in a Series of Sermons on the Shorter Catechism* (London: A. Fullarton, 1845), 155–60; Samuel Willard, *A Compleat Body of Divinity* (reprint, New York: Johnson Reprint Corp., 1969), 482–91; Herman Witsius, *The Economy of the Covenants between God & Man* (reprint, Kingsburg, Calif.: Den Dulk Christian Foundation, 1990), 1:441–68.

5. *The Workes of that Famovs and VVorthy Minister of Christ in the Vniuersitie of Cambridge, Mr. William Perkins,* 3 vols. (London: Iohn Legatt and Cantrell Ligge, 1612–13), 1:82–83, 104–105, 369–70, 430; 2:277–80; 3:154–55, 205; 138 and 382 of 2nd pagination.

6. William Bates, *The Whole Works of the Rev. W. Bates, D.D.,* ed. W. Farmer (reprint, Harrisonburg, Va.: Sprinkle, 1990, 4:299–301); Hugh Binning, *The Works of the Rev. Hugh Binning, M.A.,* ed. M. Leishman (reprint, Ligonier, Pa.: Soli Deo Gloria, 1992), 253–55; Thomas Brooks, *The Works of Thomas Brooks* (reprint, Edinburgh: Banner of Truth Trust, 2001), 4:419–20; Anthony Burgess, *Spiritual Refining: or A Treatise of Grace and Assurance* (London: A Miller for Thomas Underhill, 1652), 237–43; Stephen Charnock, *The Complete Works of Stephen Charnock* (Edinburgh: James Nichol, 1865), 3:90; George Downame, *A Treatise of Ivstification* (London: Felix Kyngston for Nicolas Bourne, 1633), 239–42; John Flavel, *The Works of John Flavel* (Edinburgh: Banner of Truth Trust, 1997), 6:197–99; Thomas Goodwin, *The Works of Thomas Goodwin* (reprint, Eureka, Calif.: Tanski, 1996), 1:83–102; William Gouge, *A Gvide to Goe to*

as Jeremiah Burroughs, Thomas Cole, Roger Drake, Thomas Hooker, Thomas Manton, Stephen Marshall, Richard Sibbes, John Tennent, and John Waite, preached one or more sermons on adoption.[7]

So significant was the Puritan emphasis on adoption that the Westminster Divines addressed it in each of their three standards. In addition to the aforementioned Chapter XII of the Westminster Confession of Faith, "Of Adoption," the Larger Catechism (Q. 74) and the Shorter Catechism (Q. 34) also address it, as have numerous commentators on the Westminster Standards ever since.[8]

God: or, An explanation of the perfect Patterne of Prayer, The Lords Prayer, 2nd ed. (London: G.M. for Edward Brewster, 1636), 10–21; Ezekiel Hopkins, *The Works of Ezekiel Hopkins,* ed. Charles W. Quick (reprint, Morgan, Pa.: Soli Deo Gloria, 1997), 2:120–21, 569–76; 3:198–99; Edward Leigh, *A Treatise of Divinity* (London, 1646), 510–11; John Owen, *The Works of John Owen,* ed. William H. Goold (reprint, London: Banner of Truth Trust, 1966), 2:207–22; 4:265–70; 23:255–76.

7. Jeremiah Burroughs, *The Saints' Happiness, Delivered in Divers Lectures on the Beatitudes* (reprint, Beaver Falls, Pa.: Soli Deo Gloria, 1988), 193–202; Thomas Cole, *A Discourse of Christian Religion, in Sundry Points…Christ the Foundation of our Adoption, from Gal. 4.5* (London: for Will. Marshall, 1698); Roger Drake, "The Believer's Dignity and Duty Laid Open, in the High Birth wherewith he is Privileged, and the Honourable Employment to which he is Called," in *Puritan Sermons 1659–1689: Being the Morning Exercises at Cripplegate, St. Giles in the Fields, and in Southwark by Seventy-five Ministers of the Gospel in or near London* (reprint, Wheaton, Ill.: Richard Owen Roberts, 1981), 5:328–44; Thomas Hooker, *The Christians Tvvo Chiefe Lessons* (reprint, Ames, Iowa: International Outreach, 2002), 159–73; Thomas Manton, *The Complete Works of Thomas Manton, D.D.* (London: James Nisbet, 1870), 1:33–57; 10:116–21; 12:111–39; Stephen Marshall, *The Works of Mr Stephen Marshall, The First Part, [section 2:] The High Priviledge of Beleevers. They are the Sons of God* (London: Peter and Edward Cole, 1661); Richard Sibbes, *Works of Richard Sibbes* (Edinburgh: Banner of Truth Trust, 2001), 4:129–49; John Tennent, "The Nature of Adoption," in *Salvation in Full Color: Twenty Sermons by Great Awakening Preachers,* ed. Richard Owen Roberts (Wheaton, Ill.: International Awakening Press, 1994), 233–50; John Waite, *Of the Creatures Liberation from the Bondage of Corruption, Wherein is Discussed…[section V]: And lastly is discussed that glorious libertie of the sonnes of God into which the creature is to be reduced* (York: Tho: Broad, 1650).

8. For example, for the Westminster Confession, see Robert Shaw, *The Reformed Faith: An Exposition of the Westminster Confession of Faith* (reprint, Inverness: Christian Focus, 1974), 137–41; for the Larger Catechism, see Thomas Ridgeley, *Commentary on the Larger Catechism* (reprint, Edmonton: Still Waters Revival Books, 1993), 2:131–37; and for the Shorter Catechism, see John Brown (of Haddington), *An Essay towards an easy, plain, practical, and extensive Explication of the Assembly's Shorter Catechism* (New York: Robert Carter & Brothers, 1849), 162–65; James Fisher, *The Assembly's Shorter Catechism Explained, by way of Question and Answer* (reprint, Lewes, East Sussex: Berith Publications, 1998), 184–87; Thomas Vincent, *The Shorter Catechism of the Westminster Assembly Explained and Proved from Scripture* (reprint, Edinburgh: Banner of

Most important, some Puritans wrote entire treatises on adoption, including:

- John Crabb, *A Testimony concerning the VVorks of the Living God. Shewing how the mysteries of his workings hath worked many wayes in and amongst mankind. Or, The knowledge of God revealed, which shews the way from the bondage of darkness into the liberty of the Sons of God.*

- Simon Ford, *The Spirit of Bondage and Adoption: Largely and Practically handled, with reference to the way and manner of working both those Effects; and the proper Cases of Conscience belonging to them both.*

- M. G., *The Glorious Excellencie of the Spirit of Adoption.*

- Thomas Granger, *A Looking-Glasse for Christians. Or, The Comfortable Doctrine of Adoption.*

- Cotton Mather, *The Sealed Servants of our God, Appearing with Two Witnesses, to produce a Well-Established Assurance of their being the Children of the Lord Almighty or, the Witness of the Holy Spirit, with the Spirit of the Beleever, to his Adoption of God; briefly and plainly Described.*

- Samuel Petto, *The Voice of the Spirit. Or, An essay towards a discoverie of the witnessings of the Spirit.*

- Samuel Willard, *The Child's Portion: Or the unseen Glory of the Children of God, Asserted, and proved: Together with several other Sermons Occasionally Preached.*[9]

Sadly, none of these books have been reprinted in recent times, which, in part, serves to promote the misconception that the Puritans rarely addressed this subject.

I ended up spending my whole summer on this topic, and found it to be one of the two most enriching studies I have engaged in in my

Truth Trust, 1980), 96–97. For additional confessional statements that address adoption, see Tim Trumper, "An Historical Study of the Doctrine of Adoption in the Calvinistic Tradition" (PhD dissertation, University of Edinburgh, 2001), 5–10.

9. Crabb (London: John Gain, 1682); Ford (London: T. Maxey, for Sa. Gellibrand, 1655); M. G. (London: Jane Coe, for Henry Overton, 1645); Granger (London: William Iones, 1620); Mather (Boston: Daniel Henchman, 1727); Petto (London: Livewell Chapman, 1654); Willard (Boston: Samuel Green, to be sold by Samuel Phillips, 1684).

lifetime. The chapter turned into a little book that proved to be trans-forming for my own soul.

In this chapter, I want to take a modified version of this Puritan study and look at it in the context of 1 John 3:1–3, trying to bring together the apostle John and his impact on the Puritans, and what the Puritans have to say to us. So this chapter will be a mixture of exegesis, historical theology, and pastoral application. If you are a believer, I hope that you will find it very beneficial for your own relationship with God and your fellow Christians.

I aim to show, first, the amazing wonder of our adoption by God; second, its Trinitarian foundation; third, its transforming power; fourth, its benefits and privileges; and fifth, its responsibili-ties and duties.

The Amazing Wonder of Adoption

The triune God delights in family planning. Unlike most modern human family planning, which is restrictive and limiting, God's plans for His family are expansive and enlarging. Spiritual adop-tion—the wonderful teaching that every genuine Christian is an adopted child in God's family—is a foundational and vital factor that God uses to fulfill His plans for His family.

The doctrine of spiritual adoption, which the Puritans defined as "an act of God's free grace, whereby we are received into the number, and have a right to all the privileges, of the sons of God" (Westmin-ster Shorter Catechism, Q. 34), is addressed in several places in the New Testament. Romans 8:14–16 and Galatians 4:4–6 may be the most familiar to us, but adoption is also a frequent theme in the first epistle of John. Particularly in 1 John 3:1–3, the apostle lays before us the central and major New Testament themes of the fatherhood of God and the corresponding sonship of believers. We do not have to read far in the New Testament before we realize that these themes are of critical importance for the entirety of the Christian life. Where there is some degree of spiritual maturity, some realization of our sonship to the heavenly Father, this Father-son relationship under-girds our prayer; indeed, it controls our entire outlook on life. Much of what Christ taught us can be summarized in the precious doctrine of the fatherhood of God. The revelation of God's fatherhood to the believer is, in a sense, the climax of the Scriptures and one of the greatest benefits of salvation.

John begins the third chapter of his first epistle with a call for believers to drop everything and consider the great doctrine of adoption. "Behold!" is John's opening cry. He is saying, "Look at this!" The apostle is so overwhelmed with the wonder of God's adoption of believers that he is determined to direct everyone's attention to it. He asks us to gaze with him upon this wonder: "Behold, what manner of love the Father hath bestowed upon us that we should be called the sons of God" (v. 1). It is as if John asks: "Do you know the wonder of this precious truth? Have you, by faith, apprehended this magnificent doctrine of adoption?"

John's sense of astonishment is more evident in the original Greek. The Greek interrogative, *potapos*, originally meant, "from what country or realm?" It later came to mean more generally, "of what sort or manner?" Matthew 8:27 uses the same idiom to express how astonished the disciples were when Jesus calmed the winds and the sea: "What manner of man is this (literally, 'from what realm does this man come?'), that even the winds and the sea obey him!"

God's adoption of believers is something unparalleled in this world. This fatherly love has come to us from another realm. The world does not understand such love, for it has never seen anything like it. It is beyond the realm of ordinary human experience.

John is astonished because God shows such amazing love even though we are by nature outcasts, rebels, and enemies to Him and His kingdom. God call us the sons of God; that is, He brings us into His family, giving us the name, the privileges, and all the blessings of His own children. He invites us to know Him as Father and to dwell under His protection and care, and to come to Him with all our cares and needs. John is overwhelmed at the thought of being received and acknowledged as a member of God's family.

Have you ever considered what a stupendous wonder adoption is? Wilhelmus à Brakel (1635–1711) put it this way: "From being a child of the devil to becoming a child of God, from being a child of wrath to becoming the object of God's favor, from a child of condemnation to becoming an heir of all the promises and a possessor of all blessings, and to be exalted from the greatest misery to the highest felicity—this is something which exceeds all comprehension and all adoration."[10]

Perkins (1558–1603) said that a believer should esteem his adoption as God's child to be greater than being "the childe or heire of any earthly Prince [since] the sonne of the greatest Potentate may be the childe of wrath: but the child of God by grace, hath Christ Iesus to bee his eldest *brother*, with whom he is *fellow heire* in heaven; hee hath the holy Ghost also for his *comforter*, and the kingdome of heauen for his euerlasting *inheritance.*" Perkins lamented how few people realize this experientially: "At earthly preferments men will stand amazed; but seldome shall you finde a man that is rauished with ioy in this, that hee is the childe of God."[11]

The Puritans believed that God's act of adoption is astonishingly comprehensive. Most Puritans placed their treatment of adoption in the *ordo salutis* between justification and sanctification, following the order set forth by the Westminster divines. Logically, that makes considerable sense, given the inevitable ties between justification and adoption, and between sanctification and adoption. Other Puritans, however, pointed out that though adoption can at times be viewed as one aspect of salvation, or one part of the *ordo salutis*, at other times it can be understood best as comprehending all of soteriology. For example, Stephen Marshall (1594–1655) writes, "Though sometimes in the holy Scriptures our Sonship is but one of our Priviledges, yet very frequently in the Scripture all the Beleevers do obtain from Christ in this world and the world to come, here and to eternity, all is comprehended in this one, *That they are made the Children of God.*" Marshall goes on to cite several examples. He writes, "I know not how often the whol Covenant of Grace is expressed in that word, *I wil be their Father, they shal be my children.*" He also invites readers to consider Ephesians 1:5, where, he says, Paul comprehends all of salvation "in this one expression, *having predestinated us to the adoption of children.*"[12] Clearly, the Puritans ascribed a lofty and comprehensive place to the amazing wonder of adoption in their soteriology.

---

10. Wilhelmus à Brakel, *The Christian's Reasonable Service*, trans. Bartel Elshout, ed. Joel R. Beeke (Grand Rapids: Reformation Heritage Books, 1999), 2:419.

11. *Workes of Perkins*, 3:138 (2nd pagination).

12. *Works of Stephen Marshall*, 37–38. Marshall also uses Romans 8:23 and the beginning of Galatians 4 to buttress Scripture's frequent comprehensive use of adoption.

Do you stand in awe at the thought of this wonderful adopting love of the Father? Holy wonder and amazement is an important part of Christian experience. One of the devil's tactics is to dull our sense of wonder, convincing us that we feel such wonder only in the initial stages of becoming a Christian. It is true that a sinner experiences a special sense of joy and wonder when he first comes to know Christ. We often refer to that time as the period of one's "first love." But John is writing here as an elderly man who has been a believer for more than sixty years. Yet his heart is still filled with amazement at being a son of God. He has never gotten beyond his initial sense of wonder at God's comprehensive fatherly love.

The Trinitarian Foundation of Adoption

Believers are not sons of God by nature because we lost the status and privileges of sonship in our tragic fall with Adam in Paradise. Adoption is possible only when God's electing grace calls us into all the privileges and blessings of being His children. When we are born again, Christ delivers us from Satan's slavery, and as grace upon grace, transfers us to the Father's sonship. God calls us sons because we are adopted into His family.

Adoption in the time of John usually took place in adolescence or adulthood, not infancy. Under Roman law, adoption was a legal act by which a man chose someone outside of his family to be the heir of his estate. Likewise, believers become children of God through the gracious act of God the Father, who makes them heirs of the kingdom of God and of His covenant. The Father seals and witnesses that "He doth make an eternal covenant of grace with us, and adopts us for His children and heirs, and therefore will provide us with every good thing, and avert all evil or turn it to our profit." Therefore, our children are also "to be baptized as heirs of the kingdom of God and of His covenant."[13]

Sometimes adopting parents announce the reception of their adopted with the words "our chosen son." Likewise, dear believer, God the Father set His heart upon you while you were a stranger and

---

13. These emphases, quoted from the Dutch Reformed liturgy for baptism (*The Psalter* [Grand Rapids: Reformation Heritage Books, 1999], 126), also come shining through in the directions of the Westminster Assembly for the administration of baptism (Westminster Larger Catechism, Q. 165–67).

rebel, and in no way a member of His family. He called you, drew you to Himself, brought you into His family, proclaimed you to be His child, and now reserves for you the eternal inheritance of the kingdom of God.

The story is told of a king who found a poor man's child, took him out of the gutter, and made him a prince in the royal household, with all its status and privilege. The gospel story is not fiction, however, for Scripture reveals that the Almighty God and Father has set His love upon you (Jer. 31:3), brought you up out of a horrible pit (Ps. 40:2), brought you into His household (Heb. 3:6), and gave you all the privileges and blessings of being His child (Rom. 8:16, 17).

"Beloved, now are we the sons of God," says John in verse 2. This is not merely legal language. We believers are, indeed, God's chosen ones, as Ephesians 1:5–7 says. How astonishing that we, as God's adopted children, share the privileges that belong to God's only begotten Son! Have you grasped the astonishing truth of what Christ prays in John 17:23: "…that the world may know that thou hast sent me, and hast loved them, as thou hast loved me"? This love is the essence of God's fatherhood. The love of the Father for the Son extends to all who are in Him, as adopted sons and daughters of God. It shows us how far God is willing to go when He adopts us into His family.

We become children of God, that is, God becomes our Father, by substitution or, as John calls it, propitiation: "Herein is love, not that we loved God, but that he loved us, and sent his Son to be the propitiation for our sins" (1 John 4:10; cf. 1 John 2:2). Propitiation may be a strange term to us, but it is a vitally important one, for it contains the heart of the gospel.

Let me explain. We are not sons and daughters of God by nature. Many live under this false idea. They think that everyone is a child of God because we all come from the same Father. It is true that we are all creatures of the one divine Creator, but the Bible nowhere tells us that we are children of God by nature. Rather, it tells us that by nature we are children of wrath (Eph. 2:3). Because of the fallen, sinful nature that we inherit from Adam, we are the objects of God's wrath, anger, and judgment. As Watson writes, "We have enough in us to move God to correct us, but nothing to move him to adopt us, therefore exalt free grace, begin the work of angels here;

bless him with your praises who hath blessed you in making you his sons and daughters."[14]

God has only one natural Son, the eternal Word who became flesh as the Lord Jesus Christ. His only begotten Son is the Son of His love. Now God's amazing love to sinners is revealed in the way He makes children of wrath to be the sons of His love. The Father loves the Son, but in the astonishing substitution that God accepted in the atoning sacrifice of Christ, the wrath of God against us was poured upon His only begotten Son, who thereby became the atoning sacrifice or propitiation for our sins. We who were sons of wrath become the sons of His love, because the beloved Son of God became the bearer of His wrath on the cross.

This is the astonishing biblical doctrine of penal substitution. Dear believers, Jesus Christ, who deserved eternal heaven, bore our eternal hell as the punishment of our sins, so that the gates of hell may be eternally closed for us and the gates of heaven be eternally thrown open. Oh, what a price Christ had to pay to accomplish this task! He had to hang in the naked flame of His Father's wrath and be cast into outer darkness, crying out, "My God, my God, why hast thou forsaken me?" (Matt. 27:46)—all so that God could, for Christ's sake, bring us, who were by nature estranged and rebellious sinners, into the family of God and acknowledge us as His children.

This is the only way to become a child of God—only through Christ as the propitiation, the atoning sacrifice, the penal substitute, the Lamb of God, delivered up for our sins. Only for Christ's sake does God become the Father of His people. What country does this love come from—a love that would cause the holy God of all eternity to accept this transaction on behalf of poor, hopeless, hell-worthy sinners such as we are?

How great is the love the Father has lavished on us that we should be called children of God—we who deserve His judgment, dethroned Him from our lives, spurned His love, and defied His laws. We can never earn God's love, yet He graciously lavishes love upon us in Christ. Here, surely, is the great assurance of the child of God, that he was not chosen for any good in him but simply because God the Father loved him even when he was bound for hell (Rom. 5:8). God loved the sinner who had no thought of God in his heart,

14. Watson, *A Body of Divinity*, 160.

and God adopted him to be His son. How wonderful is the assurance of the Father's words: "I have loved thee with an everlasting love" (Jer. 31:3)!

All the persons of the Trinity are involved in our adoption. Adoption is the gracious act of God the Father whereby He chooses us, calls us to Himself, and gives us the privileges and blessings of His children. God the Son earned those blessings for us through His propitiatory death and sacrifice, by which we become children of God (1 John 4:10). And the Holy Spirit changes us from children of wrath, which we are by nature, into children of God by means of regeneration, or the new birth, sealing our adoption with His own witness.

Transformed Relationships Resulting from Adoption

Adoption brings blessings into every part of a believer's life. It affects his relationship to God, to the world, to his future, to himself, and to his brothers and sisters in God's family. Thus, the biblical doctrine of adoption is central to a proper understanding of every important aspect of the Christian's life. The Puritans would agree with Packer: "Sonship must be the controlling thought—the normative category, if you like—at every point."[15] All relationships are put into their proper context only when believers grasp what God has done in adopting them as His children.

Christ Himself is the best proof of this truth. Jesus' consciousness of His unique sonship with the Father controlled all of His living and thinking. As Jesus says in John 5:30, "I seek not mine own will, but the will of the Father which hath sent me," and in John 10:30, "I and my Father are one." "If I do not the works of my Father, believe me not," Jesus says in John 10:37, and, "As my Father hath sent me, even so send I you" (John 20:21). More than thirty times in the Gospel of John, Jesus speaks of God as "my Father."

Though the relationship of God the Father and God the Son is an obvious truth in the Gospels, what is not so obvious is how Jesus urges His disciples to let their thoughts and lives be controlled by the conviction that God is now their Father and they are His children. Jesus repeatedly cites sonship with the Father as the foundation of Christian discipleship. He tells His disciples that they are to be examples of trusting in their Father, enjoining them, "Take no thought, saying,

---

15. Packer, *Knowing God*, 190.

What shall we eat? or, What shall we drink? or, Wherewithal shall we be clothed?…for your heavenly Father knoweth that ye have need of all these things" (Matt. 6:31–32). The disciples' whole lives must be directed to glorifying their Father in heaven and doing His will, so Jesus teaches them to pray: "Our Father which art in heaven, Hallowed be thy name. Thy kingdom come. Thy will be done in earth, as it is in heaven" (vv. 9–10). The child of God is to live his whole life in relation to his Father, remembering that the Father has promised to give him His kingdom.

Practically speaking, the significance of adoption has great implications, as the New England Puritan John Cotton (1584–1652) particularly shows us. Our adoption transforms the following:

Our relationship to God
When the gospel breaks in upon us, we are led by the Spirit to discover the amazing truth that God is now our Father in Christ Jesus. The heartbeat of daily Christian experience is to live in fellowship with the Father and with the Son. A true Christian lives under God's fatherly love, wisdom, care, guidance, and discipline.

People are hungry for security today. They look for it in all kinds of places and things, but they often go about it the wrong way. The only place in the universe where true security can be found is in the household of the heavenly Father, who is the God and Father of our Lord Jesus Christ. There is no security outside of fellowship with God the Father through the Lord Jesus Christ in the Holy Spirit.

Many people are discovering that things that once gave them security are now failing them. They are facing failure in business or employment, or in relationships with family members and friends. The human race is beset with crises and catastrophes caused by terrorism, war, disease, famine, and death. Life is uncertain; the very ground under our feet is crumbling away. The most powerful corporation on earth may fold in the next recession. We learn that nothing in life is secure except God. He alone does not change (Mal. 3:6; Heb. 13:8).

Are you looking for security in the fatherhood of God? Are you daily being led deeper into the experience of His faithfulness as your Father? Jesus taught His disciples this truth in many ways. For example, He urged His followers to think about God's fatherly love by comparing it to the love of human fathers. He said in Matthew 7:11, "If ye then, being evil, know how to give good gifts unto your children, how much more shall your Father which is in heaven give good things to them that ask him?"

The comparison is between earthly fathers, who are evil (i.e., they have fallen natures, with flaws, failures, and sins), and the heavenly Father, who is goodness itself, and whose love never falters or changes, even when we sin against Him. God's fatherhood is flawless, in spite of our shortcomings that compel us to confess with Cotton: "Surely I am not a child of God, because I find much pride in my heart, and much rebellion and corruption in my spirit. Surely if I were born of Christ, I should be like him. But what says St. John here? We are the sons of God even now, though there is much unbelief in our hearts, and much weakness and many corruptions within us."[16] Even so, Jesus shows us that our heavenly Father's love toward us is eternal, expansive, and glorious beyond imagination.

I do not know what your experience of human fatherhood has been. Some of us had no real relationships with our earthly fathers at all; some had or have good relationships with our fathers, and others had or have disappointing, even bitter, ones. Everything that fails in human fatherhood is corrected in God's fatherhood. Everything good we experience in human fatherhood is a mere shadow of the full and perfect fatherhood of God.

If you are a father, you know how your heart sometimes aches and cries out with love for your children. Imagine multiplying that love by infinity. Then realize how even that falls short of the love of God for His people. Have you yielded to the embrace of your heavenly Father? Oh that you would allow yourself to partake of His immeasurable fatherly love!

To increase His people's appreciation for God's fatherhood, Jesus urges them to think of His own relationship to God the Father. We need to ponder the wonder of this, especially in the context of daily afflictions, remembering that Jesus experienced His Father's love even while undergoing daily afflictions in this life. When you are under God's discipline and He is permitting trials to fall upon you, remember that these difficulties are evidence of your Father's love

---

16. John Cotton, *An Exposition of First John* (reprint, Evansville, Ind.: Sovereign Grace Publishers, 1962), 319.

(Heb. 12:5–11). As a loving Father, God has a plan, a purpose, a vision for His people that embraces every affliction and heartache, every trial and hardship.

As parents, we dream of what our children might become when they grow up. Likewise, God has a vision for His children. He knows precisely what He wants them to be and become. He knows how He will mold and train them according to His plan, and inevitably, that involves discipline, because God will not permit His children to be less than what He intends them to be. He uses His fatherly discipline for their welfare (Lam. 3:31–33; Heb. 12:10). If we are born-again believers, we must ask for wisdom to see everything in our lives as coming not by chance, but from the hand of God our Father, who has adopted us as His own children.

Our relationship to the world

The believer's adoption by God the Father also affects his relationship to the world. First John 3:1b tells us that this relationship is a troubled one: "Therefore the world knoweth us not, because it knew him not." On the one hand, the believer shares with Jesus the infinite, eternal, and unchanging love of the Father, but on the other hand, he shares with Jesus the hostility, estrangement, and hatred of the world. The reason the world does not know (recognize or acknowledge) the children of God is because it does not know Jesus.

The world is baffled by what happens to God's people, for it cannot understand why they love what they love and hate what they hate. This reaction of the world is another evidence of the believer's adoption into God's family, for the world did not know Jesus either: "He came unto his own, and his own received him not" (John 1:11). He was in the world that He had created, but the world did not recognize or receive Him as the Son of God. Ultimately, it crucified Him. "If God saw it meet that his Son should be thus afflicted in the world and drink of such a bitter portion of God's wrath," writes Cotton, "let us not think we shall go to heaven and partake of those heavenly mansions which Christ has prepared for us, without also drinking of the same cup that he drank of. Let us account ourselves happy that God will so esteem us as to make us his sons."[17]

---

17. Cotton, *First John*, 318.

When a sinner is born again and brought into God's family, he comes to know the great blessings of deliverance in Christ. But the believer also discovers that worldly people no longer understand him. For example, when God converted me at age fourteen, I had to break some of my closest friendships to remain faithful to God. One friend was puzzled. "I thought I knew you, but I do not know what has happened to you," he said. "I cannot understand you. Suddenly we are living in two different worlds."

Believers and unbelievers do live in different worlds, in different kingdoms, in different families. That cannot help but have serious consequences. But adoption into God's family means that we must be willing, for Christ's sake, to live as His followers in the world even if we are misunderstood, rejected, despised, and hated, all the while giving no unnecessary offense to the world.

Our relationship to the future
John goes on to say, "Beloved, now are we the sons of God, and it doth not yet appear what we shall be: but we know that, when he shall appear, we shall be like him; for we shall see him as he is" (1 John 3:2). The prospects for God's adopted family are great, for His children will receive a glorious inheritance. They cannot even imagine the extent of that inheritance. God keeps that hidden, says Cotton, so that they may (1) be like their suffering Head, (2) have their faith exercised and be watchful, and (3) be tolerated to some degree in this world, for "if God should allow them to be perfectly holy in this world, the men of the world would not allow them to live among them long (Deut. 7:22)."[18]

Here and now, in this world, we are God's children, even though the world does not understand us. But we have something much greater in store for us—the infinite riches in glory that God the Father has laid up for us in Christ Jesus. God's child is like a poor peasant who has been taken out of the mire and raised to the position of a prince of the realm. The adopted prince lives in the palace, has free access to the king, and enjoys the king's favor, love, and protection. The prince tells the king he cannot comprehend the greatness of the king's love. It is unspeakably great to him. The king responds: "You

18. Cotton, *First John*, 320–21.

have not begun to see the extent of it. What you have now is only a foretaste. Your inheritance is still coming to you."

If our present privileges as God's adopted children are so great that the world cannot grasp them, our future prospects are so glorious that even we cannot grasp them. As 1 Corinthians 2:9 says, "Eye hath not seen, nor ear heard, neither have entered into the heart of man, the things which God hath prepared for them that love him." Because God is our Father and we are His adopted children, we have a full inheritance awaiting us. The best is yet to be. Today we experience great blessings, despite our infirmities and sins, but one day we shall be received up into glory, free from sin and in perfect communion with God. Our heavenly Father keeps the best surprises for His children until the end, when He shall turn all their sorrow into joy.

Likewise, today we look at Christ by faith. Though what we see is shadowy and dim (as "through a glass, darkly," 1 Cor. 13:12), we are being changed from glory to glory by the Spirit of the Lord (2 Cor. 3:18). One day all shadows will be removed. We will see Christ as He is, in all His glory. Moreover, God is shaping us to share in the glories of our Lord Jesus Christ. As 1 John 3:2 says, "When he shall appear, we shall be like him; for we shall see him as he is." God is changing us now, but then we shall be so changed that we will fully bear His image without spot or wrinkle. Paul tells us in Romans 8:19–23 that the whole creation waits for the day when the inheritance of the children of God will be given to them. What a future!

Our relationship to ourselves
The children of the heavenly Father know His will and purpose for them. Every adopted child of God also knows that holiness is an important part of God's purpose for his happiness in God's family. As 1 John 3:3 says, "And every man that hath this hope in him purifieth himself, even as he is pure."

In holiness, the child of God identifies himself with his Father's purposes. Sometimes children resent their father's purposes, but the true adopted son of God identifies with his Father's purpose for him. He does not try to find himself apart from his Father in heaven, but in his Father's will. Because seeking God's purposes for one's life is inseparable from the pursuit of holiness, the believer gives himself to the purpose that his Father has for him.

John tells us, "Every man that hath this hope in him purifieth himself" (3:3). So we are to purify ourselves daily, "[laying] aside every weight, and the sin which doth so easily beset us" (Heb. 12:1). As Colossians 3 tells us, holiness means putting off everything that is dishonoring to our Father, who has loved us, and to the Savior, who died to save us. It means putting on "mercies, kindness, humbleness of mind, meekness, longsuffering" (3:12). Purifying ourselves involves "the whole man," says Cotton, including what we do with our minds, affections, wills, thoughts, tongues, eyes, hands, disappointments, injuries, and enemies.[19] Purifying ourselves involves loving all that the Father loves and hating all that the Father hates. From the moment of conversion to the time we take our final breath, we have one pursuit: to purify ourselves before our Father in order to be more like Christ.

The Greek word for "purify" refers to being restored to undivided allegiance or having one's eyes on one thing. It means praying as David prayed, "Unite my heart to fear thy name" (Ps. 86:11c). It implies wholeness and singleness of purpose, the very opposite of being "doubled minded" (James 1:8). It means having undivided motives in our living and our service, being wholly dedicated to living to glorify Jesus Christ. Christians become known as sons of God because they have a new goal for themselves, a new relationship toward themselves. By God's grace, they purify themselves even as Christ is pure.

Our relationship to the family of God
If we rightly understand that we have been adopted into God's family (note the usage of the plural throughout 1 John 3:1–2), our attitude toward our brothers and sisters in the family will also be affected (3:14–18). We have not been adopted to live apart from that family but to live within it. God's purpose in adopting children is to create a household or family, that reflects His gracious purpose that will one day be fulfilled in heaven. He wants the love that exists between the Father, the Son, and the Holy Spirit to be extended through the love between brothers and sisters in Christ. As Cotton says, "The sons of

---

19. Cotton, *First John*, 331.

God ought to be the men of our love and delight (3 John 1, 2, 5; 1 Pet. 2:11; Phil. 4:1)."[20]

The communion of saints is essential to the gospel. That is why it is so grievous when people in the church do not show love to one another. If we profess a Savior who in love laid down His life for us, and claim that we are part of His family, we ought to be willing to lay down our lives for other members of that family. We should uphold them, love them, and sacrifice for them. We should not grieve each other, wound each other, or gossip about each other. The way we behave toward other Christians proves whether or not we are adopted children of God (3:14–15). We are to love fellow adoptees of God, Cotton says, because of (1) "God's singular love to them," (2) "their love to God," and (3) "the truth that is in every Christian believer (2 John 1, 2)."[21]

If we show little love to other children of God, we prove that we have tasted little of God's love in our lives, for those who have experienced much love from Him cannot help but love others. Those who have not tasted the love of God will not love the brethren. As Cotton concludes, "The lack of love to any of our brethren is a sign of abiding in the state of damnation, or in an unregenerate and carnal state."[22]

The Benefits and Privileges of Adoption

The Puritans spend more time expounding what are variously called the privileges, liberties, benefits, blessings, or rights of adoption than any other aspect of this doctrine. This preoccupation is also evident in the Westminster Confession of Faith (XII) and Larger Catechism (Q. 74), where more than half of the presentation of adoption is devoted to a listing of these "liberties and privileges," each of which the Spirit uses to exercise His transforming power in the lives of God's children, to their comfort.

The greatest privilege can best be summarized as *heirship*. God's adopted children are all royal heirs-apparent and co-heirs with Christ (Rom. 8:16–17). "Men may have many children yet but one is an heir," writes Burroughs. "But all the children of God are heirs."[23]

---

20. Cotton, *First John*, 316.
21. Cotton, *First John*, 317.
22. Cotton, *First John*, 372.
23. Burroughs, *The Saints' Happiness*, 192.

They are, as Hebrews 12:23 calls them, "the firstborn, which are written in heaven."

The Puritans make much of joint-heirship with Christ. As co-heirs with Christ, believers share in Christ's kingship, and therefore partake of the kingdom of heaven as their inheritance. Believers are made kings to the Father in His spiritual kingdom in three respects, writes Granger. "1. Because they are Lords and Conquerors of their enemies, Sinne, Satan, the World, Death, Hell. 2. They are partakers of the kingdome of Christ and of saluation; for wee haue receiued of Christ grace for grace, and glorie for glorie. 3. They haue interest, dominion, and soueraigntie of all things by Christ."[24] Witsius stresses that "all things" includes the right of "possession of the whole world," which was given to but lost by Adam (Gen. 1:28; 3:24), promised to Abraham (Rom. 4:13), and repurchased by Christ for "himself and his brethren," so that now all things, both present and to come, are His people's.[25] Ultimately, believers are lords and possessors of all things, because they belong to Christ, who belongs to God (1 Cor. 3:21–23).[26]

Nothing in this world can match the inheritance of believers. It knows no *corruption* (1 Peter 1:4)—not "by outward principles, as fire, violence, &c.; nor by inward principles, as sin and other taints which defile" (1 Peter 1:18). It has no *succession*. The heavenly Father and His children always live out of the same inheritance, so believers' inheritance is as unchangeable as Christ's priesthood (Heb. 7:24). It faces no *division*. Every heir enjoys the whole inheritance, since God is both "infinite and indivisible." "God gives his all, not half, but his whole kingdom" (Gen. 25:5; Rev. 21:7).[27]

Specific blessings that accrue to us as believers from His divine inheritance and spiritual adoption include the most wonderful privileges one could ever imagine, both in this world and in the world to come. Here is a summary of them, drawn from the Puritans:

- Our Father cuts us off from the family to which we naturally belong in Adam as children of wrath and of the devil,

---

24. Granger, *A Looking-Glasse for Christians*, 26.

25. Witsius, *Economy of the Covenants*, 1:452–53.

26. *Workes of Perkins*, 1:82, 369.

27. Drake, *Puritan Sermons*, 5:334; cf. *Works of Owen*, 2:218–21; Burroughs, *The Saints' Happiness*, 196.

and ingrafts us into His own family to make us members of the covenant family of God. "Adoption translates us out of a miserable estate, into a happy estate," writes Cole. "God is in covenant with us, and we in him."[28]

- Our Father gives us freedom to call upon Him as our Father and gives us a new name, which serves as our guarantee of admission to the house of God as sons and daughters of God (Rev. 2:17; 3:12). We are a peculiar people—"[His] people, which are called by [His] name" (2 Chron. 7:14). That means, says Boston, that our "old name is for ever laid aside. [We] are no more called children of the devil, but the sons and daughters of God" (Heb. 12:5–8).[29] Cotton goes a step further, saying expressly that this name is *Adoption*: "[We] have this white Stone, that is Absolution for sin, and in that a new name written, that is, Adoption: and if we be of a meek, humble, innocent, frame of mind, we have this comfort."[30] By the Spirit of adoption, we have access to God as a reconciled Father through Christ. We have liberty to call God our Father, which "is more worth than a thousand worlds" (Jer. 3:4).[31]

- Our Father gifts us with the Spirit of adoption. Believers are, by grace, partakers of the Holy Spirit. This Spirit, Burroughs tells us, enlightens our minds, sanctifies our hearts, makes God's wisdom and will known to us, guides us to eternal life, works the entire work of salvation in us, and seals it to us unto the day of redemption (Eph. 4:30).[32]

- Our Father restores us to likeness to Himself and His Son. The Father imparts to His children a filial heart and disposition that resemble His own. Drake writes, "All God's adopted children bear their Father's image, as Gideon's brethren did his (Judg. 8:18). They are like God, in holiness [and] in dignity" (Matt. 5:44–45; Rom. 8:29; Heb. 2:7; 1 John 3:2–3).[33]

---

28. Cole, *Christ the Foundation of our Adoption*, 351.
29. *The Complete Works of the Late Rev. Thomas Boston, Ettrick,* ed. Samuel M'Millan (reprint, Wheaton, Ill.: Richard Owen Roberts, 1980), 1:624.
30. Quoted in Jesper Rosenmeir, "'Clearing the Medium': A Reevaluation of the Puritan Plain Style in Light of John Cotton's *A Practicall Commentary Upon the First Epistle Generall of John," William and Mary Quarterly* 37, 4 (1980): 582.
31. *Works of Boston*, 1:623.
32. Burroughs, *The Saints' Happiness*, 196.
33. Drake, "The Believer's Dignity and Duty Laid Open," in *Puritan Sermons*, 5:333.

- Our Father especially strengthens our faith through His gifts of promises and prayer. "If we are adopted," writes Watson, "then we have an interest in all the promises: the promises are children's bread." They are like a garden, Watson goes on to say, in which some herb is found to cure every ailment.[34] Or, as William Spurstowe put it, God's promises are like a bag full of coins that He unties and pours out at the feet of His adopted children, saying, "Take what you will."[35]

  Concerning prayer, we are given limitless access to our heavenly Father. Children have the right of access to their father, no matter how busy or important he is—even if he is president of the nation. Even so, in the New Testament, adopted sons are encouraged to come boldly to the throne of grace in and through the God-man Savior to obtain mercy and find grace to help in time of need (Heb. 4:14–16), notwithstanding the exaltedness of their God. The Spirit teaches us that the Father in heaven is more pleased to see His adopted children come through the door of prayer into His throne room than we are pleased to see our children come through the door into our living room. Willard writes that the Spirit "enlivens" the faith of believers, enabling them "to Go to God as a Father, and claim this relation, and upon the claim, believingly to plead with him for the acceptance of their persons, the audience of their Prayers, the granting of their requests, and supplying of all their wants" (Rom. 8:15).[36]

- Our Father corrects and chastens us for our sanctification: "He chasteneth, and scourgeth every son whom he receiveth" (Heb. 12:6). All chastisements involve discipline that comes from our Father's hand and works together for our best welfare (2 Sam. 7:14; Ps. 89:32–33; Rom. 8:28, 36–37; 2 Cor. 12:7). Our sufferings are "for our education and instruction in his family," writes Owen;[37] or, as Willard puts it, "All our afflictions are helps toward heaven." They contribute to the "increase of [believers'] eternal glory: every reproach and injury doth

---

34. Watson, *A Body of Practical Divinity*, 160.

35. William Spurstowe, *The Wells of Salvation Opened: or A Treatise discovering the nature, preciousness, and usefulness, of the Gospel Promises, and Rules for the Right Application of them* (London: T. R. & E. M. for Ralph Smith, 1655), 34ff.

36. Willard, *The Child's Portion*, 21.

37. *Works of Owen*, 16:257.

but add weight to their Crown."[38] We may foolishly think that God chastens us to destroy us, but 1 Corinthians 11:32 teaches us, "We are chastened of the Lord, that we should not be condemned with the world."[39]

- Our Father comforts us with His love and pity, and moves us to rejoice in intimate communion with Him and His Son (Ps. 103:13; Rom. 5:5). He does that in several ways, as Willard notes: "He applies the precious promises to [believers'] souls, he gives them cordials of comfort, communicates unto them the sips and foretastes of glory, [and] fills them with inward joys and refreshings."[40] The Father commends and encourages us even for the smallest act of obedience.[41] He comforts us in accord with the afflictions He has measured out for us.[42]

- Our Father offers us spiritual freedom as His sons and daughters (John 8:36). This liberty releases us from bondage (Gal. 4:7). It delivers us from the slavish subjection, the servile pedagogy, the condemning power, the intolerable yoke, and the thundering curses of the law as a covenant of works (Gal. 3:13), though not from the law's regulating power.[43]

Christian liberty delivers us from the impugning, condemning, and reigning power of sin (2 Cor. 5:19; Rom. 8:1; 6:12), making possible the enjoyment of peace with God as His children. But that liberty must not be abused. As Cole writes, "'Tis a dangerous thing to speak too freely of Christian Liberty, because many under that pretence, allow themselves in very unwarrantable courses, running into excess, laying aside all Moderation."[44]

Spiritual liberty delivers us from the world and all its powerful temptations, persecutions, and threatenings (1 John 5:4). It delivers us from the bondage of Satan, from hypocrisy and anxiety, and from the doctrines and traditions of men, so that we may freely bind ourselves to the teaching of God. It grants us liberty to live transparently before God, to serve and love

38. Willard, *The Child's Portion*, 28.
39. *Workes of Perkins*, 1:82; Willard, *The Child's Portion*, 18–19; Granger, *A Looking-Glasse for Christians*, 31–32.
40. Willard, *The Child's Portion*, 22.
41. Willard, *The Child's Portion*, 19.
42. *Workes of Perkins*, 1:369.
43. *Works of Boston*, 1:625; Cole, *Christ the Foundation of our Adoption*, 352–53.
44. Cole, *Christ the Foundation of our Adoption*, 355.

Him, and to walk in His ways with heart, mind, and strength (Ps. 18:1), so that we gladly take His yoke upon us and serve Him with filial obedience each day (1 Peter 1:14), confessing, "This is my Father's world."[45]

- Our Father preserves us and keeps us from falling (Ps. 91:11–12; 1 Peter 1:5). He restores us from every backsliding way, recovering and humbling us, always preventing our hypocrisy.[46] Willard says, "Gods Sons in this life are like little Children, always tripping, and stumbling, and falling, and so weak that they could never get up again but for him: but by reasons of his hand that is upon them, his everlasting Arm that is under them."[47]

- Our Father sends forth His angels as ministering spirits, to serve us for good (Ps. 34:7; Heb. 1:14).[48] They guard us and watch for us. Willard calls them "tutelary Angels" who guard and defend us from evil, and watch for our good (Ps. 91:11). "They pitch their tents round about [believers], *Psal.* 34.1, they bring down messages of peace from heaven, even answers of their Prayers, *Dan.* 9.23, strengthen and confirm them in their secret conflicts, *Luk.* 22.43, and when they come to die, they are a convoy to carry their Souls home to eternal rest, *Luk.* 16.22."[49]

- Our Father provides everything that we need as His children, both physically and spiritually (Ps. 34:10; Matt. 6:31–33), and averts all evil or turns it to our profit. He defends us from our enemies—Satan, the world, and our own flesh—and rights our wronged cause. He assists and strengthens us, always lending us a helping hand to carry us through every difficulty and temptation (2 Tim. 4:17). We may safely leave everything in His fatherly hands, knowing that He will never leave us or forsake us (Heb. 13:5–6).

---

45. Willard, *The Child's Portion*, 23–27.

46. Ridgeley, *Commentary on the Larger Catechism*, 2:136.

47. Willard, *The Child's Portion*, 17.

48. *Workes of Perkins*, 1:83, 369.

49. Willard, *The Child's Portion*, 27–28; Granger, *A Looking-Glasse for Christians*, 30–31.

The Responsibilities and Duties of Adoption

Then, too, adoption imposes *responsibilities and duties* on God's children. The Puritans taught that every privilege of adoption has a corresponding responsibility or duty, each of which transforms the way believers think and live. These may be summarized as follows:

- Break off all former family ties. Just as you cannot be married to two women at once, you cannot belong to two families at once. If you are adopted, you must break off your allegiance to the world and give all your allegiance to your Father and to your new brothers and sisters.

- Trust your Father's Word. "Trust in the LORD with all thine heart; and lean not unto thine own understanding" (Prov. 3:5). You owe that trust to God. He is so good to you. Has He ever failed you? With hindsight, has He ever given you one affliction you did not need? Trust Him, trust His Word, trust His providence, and trust His engagements with you.

- Engage in your Father's work. You are to be about your Father's business, like your Elder Brother, remembering that the night is coming when no man can work (Luke 2:49, John 9:4). Do what you can in this life to glorify your Father. Your Father does not need you to help Him. He can do all things without our aid. Perhaps you remember when your children were very young and asked whether they could help you with something; you said yes because you wanted them to be involved. It actually took more time to do the task than if you had done it alone, but you said: "I want you to help, my son, my daughter. I want to train you to work at my side." That is what our Father does with us. He could do everything miraculously in one moment without means, but He is patient with us as we stumble along. Be engaged in your Father's world and in your Father's work.

- Be tolerant of your Father's family in non-essential differences. Remember, as Charles H. Spurgeon said, in heaven we will all find out there were a number of things wrong in our heads, even though our hearts were made right. All our head errors will be straightened out. So here, too, remember that not everyone will see eye to eye with you on non-essentials, but it is all right if you love the Lord Jesus Christ in sincerity. Be tolerant without sacrificing the essentials of the faith.

- Show childlike reverence and love for your Father in everything. Reflect habitually upon your Father's great glory and
  majesty. Stand in awe of Him; render Him honor, praise, and
  thanksgiving in all things. Remember, your holy Father sees
  everything. Children sometimes commit dreadful acts in the
  absence of their parents, but your Father is never absent.

- Submit to your Father in every providence. When He visits
  you with the rod, do not resist or murmur. Do not react by saying, "'I fear that I am not a child of God, God is not my Father,
  because God deals harshly with me; if He were my Father,
  He would have compassion on me; He would then deliver me
  from this grievous and especially this sinful cross'—to speak
  thus does not befit the nature of an upright child," writes
  Brakel. Rather, "it is fitting for a child to be quiet, to humbly
  submit, and to say, 'I will bear the indignation of the LORD,
  because I have sinned against him'" (Mic. 7:9).[50]

  Burgess says: "If thou hadst a Child-like disposition, thou
  wouldst say, although all I feel be bitter, yet he is a Father still.
  I have been an ill Child, and this makes him a Good Father
  in chastising."[51]

- Obey and imitate your Father, and love His image-bearers.
  Strive to be like Him, to be holy as He is holy, to be loving as
  He is loving. We are to be followers ("imitators") of God (Eph.
  5:1) to show that we bear the family likeness.

  We are, then, to love the Father's image wherever we see it
  in our fellow believers. Willard writes, "The Saints are living
  Images of the Lord, we may see in them, not only the likeness
  to, but the shining reflection of his communicated perfec-
  tions: Hence we should love the Saints."[52] We are to live as
  God's children in mutual love and patience with each other,
  having the same Father, Elder Brother, and indwelling Spirit.

- Rejoice in being in your Father's presence. Delight in communing with Him. Burgess writes, "A Son delights to have letters
  from his Father, to have discourse about him, especially to
  enjoy his presence."[53] Resist every hindrance, therefore, that
  keeps you from relishing your Father's adopting grace.

50. Brakel, *The Christian's Reasonable Service*, 2:437.
51. Burgess, *Spiritual Refining*, 239.
52. Willard, *The Child's Portion*, 43.
53. Burgess, *Spiritual Refining*, 240.

In heaven, this joy will be full; our adoption will then be perfected (Rom. 8:23). Then we will enter into the Father's "presence and palace," where we will be "everlastingly enjoying, delighting, and praising God."[54] Let us hope and long for that, as children who eagerly anticipate our full inheritance, where the triune God shall be our all in all.[55]

Concluding Applications

The Puritans teach us a great deal more about spiritual adoption and its transforming power, blessings, and responsibilities than is usually acknowledged today. They teach us the importance of fleeing from sin and pursuing a conscious sense of our adoption.[56] They show us, as Packer helpfully summarizes, that our adoption helps us better grasp the ministry of the Holy Spirit, the power of gospel holiness, our own assurance of faith, the solidity of the Christian family, and the glory of the Christian hope.[57]

The Puritans also warn us of the danger of remaining members of Satan's family—especially while under the means of grace. "Many a gospel-call has sounded in your ears, sinner," writes Boston; "hast thou not come away on the call? Then thou art yet a child of the devil, Acts xiii. 10. and therefore an heir of hell and of wrath." When the unbeliever objects, Boston responds: "Whose image dost thou bear? Holiness is God's image, unholiness the devil's. Thy dark heart and unholy life plainly tell the family thou art of."[58]

As strongly as the Puritans admonish, so strongly they invite and encourage. Willard writes: "What do you think of it, who have been often invited in the Gospel to embrace [Christ]? Will not [adoption] present him before you as one worth the entertaining? Receive him by a true Faith, and he will make you, not only Friends, but Children unto God."[59]

Above all, the Puritans use the truth of adoption to transform God's needy children by affording them powerful comforts. Hooker

54. *Works of Manton*, 12:125.
55. Drake, *Puritan Sermons*, 5:342; cf. Willard, *The Child's Portion*, 71.
56. *Workes of Perkins*, 3:205.
57. Packer, *Knowing God*, 198–207.
58. *Works of Boston*, 1:627; cf. Mather, *The Sealed Servants of our God*, 23–28.
59. Willard, *The Child's Portion*, 34–42; cf. Mather, *The Sealed Servants of our God*, 28–36.

shows how adoption comforts them in the face of the sight and sense of their unworthiness, outward poverty, the contempt of the world, infirmities, afflictions, persecutions, and dangers.[60] When oppressed with sin, buffeted by Satan, enticed by the world, or alarmed by fears of death, the Puritans encourage believers to take refuge in their precious heavenly Father, saying with Willard: "Am I not still a Child? And if so, then I am sure, that though he correct me (and I deserve it, nor will I refuse to submit my self patiently unto it) yet he cannot take away his loving kindness from me."[61]

Willard concludes: "Be always comforting of your selves with the thoughts of your Adoption: Draw your comforts at this tap, fetch your consolations from this relation; be therefore often chewing upon the precious priviledges of it, and make them your rejoicing. Let this joy out-strip the verdure of every other joy. Let this joy dispel the mists of every sorrow, and clear up your souls in the midst of all troubles and difficulties" as you await heavenly glory, where you will live out your perfect adoption by forever communing with the triune God. There you will "dwel at the fountain, and swim for ever in those bankless, and bottomless Oceans of Glory."[62]

---

60. Hooker, *The Christians Tvvo Chiefe Lessons*, 170–74.
61. Willard, *The Child's Portion*, 51–52.
62. Willard, *The Child's Portion*, 54, 66–70.

**RESTING IN
THE FATHER'S
LOVING
HANDS**

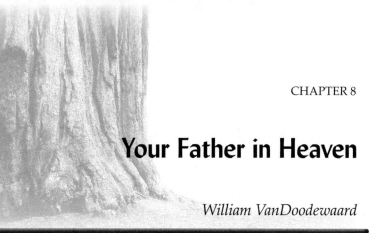

CHAPTER 8

Your Father in Heaven

William VanDoodewaard

> *Ye have heard that it hath been said, Thou shalt love thy neighbour, and hate thine enemy. But I say unto you, Love your enemies, bless them that curse you, do good to them that hate you, and pray for them which despitefully use you, and persecute you; that ye may be the children of your Father which is in heaven.... Be ye therefore perfect, even as your Father which is in heaven is perfect.*
>
> —Matthew 5:43–48

What is our Lord Jesus Christ teaching us about God the Father in the Sermon on the Mount (Matthew 5–7)? What impact should this have on our hearts and lives? In this chapter, rather than focusing on a single passage, I want to listen more widely to the Sermon on the Mount, following a specific, revealed theme.

Martin Lloyd-Jones states, "It is important for us to take the Sermon on the Mount as a whole before we come to the details…[there] is this constant danger of 'missing the [forest] because of the trees.'… The Sermon on the Mount, if I may use such a comparison, is like a great musical composition, a symphony…the whole is greater than a collection of the parts, and we must never lose sight of this wholeness."[1] So before we turn to examine the theme of God the Father, we will consider its context in the Sermon on the Mount as a whole.

The Sermon on the Mount
We know from the Gospels that our Lord Jesus Christ had already been teaching and preaching "the gospel of the kingdom"; He had

---

1. Martyn Lloyd-Jones, *Studies in the Sermon on the Mount* (Grand Rapids: Eerdmans, 2000), 22.

been calling men, women, and children to "repent: for the kingdom of heaven is at hand" (Matt. 4:17), revealing Himself as the Christ, the Savior, the One who is willing and able to forgive sins (Mark 2:5, 9–11), bringing new life and reconciliation with God. In John 6:40, He declares, "This is the will of him that sent me, that everyone which seeth the Son, and believeth on him, may have everlasting life."

In the Gospel of Matthew, we see Jesus going up onto the mountain, followed by the crowds. He sits down, gathers His disciples around Him, and begins to teach. This is a great fulfillment of the Old Testament's Mount Sinai: with crowds surrounding him, Moses the go-between goes up onto the mountain, and God speaks to him. God delivers the law in the context of the covenant of grace: "I am the LORD thy God, which have brought thee out of the land of Egypt" (Ex. 20:2).

Jesus is also a go-between, but much greater than Moses. He is the Prophet, the Preacher, the Mediator, the God-man, the Eternal Son, God with us. Jesus Christ as Immanuel, the Savior, speaks to His disciples and the gathered people as the living Word made flesh. Jesus speaks and preaches with unique authority and power. We know this from the end of the sermon: "And it came to pass, when Jesus had ended these sayings, the people were astonished at his doctrine: For he taught them as one having authority, and not as the scribes" (Matt. 7:28–29).

What does our Lord proclaim with such authority? It is the high claim of God on the lives of men and women, the high calling of the Christian life. He proclaims true holiness and goodness in a way that probes the depths of our hearts. He magnifies God's law, showing God's perfect goodness and holiness. Through it all, Jesus points us to the Father—at least twenty times directly. Look with me at how our Lord Jesus reveals the Father to us.

"Your Father" Revealed
Giving glory to your Father
Jesus' first reference to God the Father in the Gospel of Matthew comes in 5:16: "Let your light so shine before men, that they may see your good works, and glorify your Father which is in heaven." Prior to this, when Jesus was baptized, a voice from heaven—the Father's voice—said, "This is my beloved Son, in whom I am well pleased"

(Matt. 3:17). What is perhaps most amazing in chapter 5 is that Jesus is saying "My Father" is "your Father."

He says that His hearers are to let their light shine before others in order that their good works may be evident and bring glory to the Father. Yet who is Jesus encouraging to be witnesses by doing good and so giving glory to their Father? Who is He preaching to as He proclaims these words? He is preaching to a broad audience that includes His disciples and the gathered crowds—most of them undoubtedly drawn from the Old Testament covenantal people of God. They are undoubtedly a mixed crowd, believers and unbelievers—even the disciples sitting at His feet (cf. John 6:70). Christ, the eternal Son, the Word made flesh, as the Messiah and Redeemer of His people, by His Word graciously and profoundly calls them all to live holy lives, to do good, and to give glory to their Father in heaven—things they can do only in and through Himself, by coming to Him and living in repentance and faith. Lloyd-Jones comments, "It is only those who are in the Lord Jesus Christ who are truly the children of God."[2] David Dickson says that "no good work can be done *except by a child of God*, in obedience to his God and Father's command, for the good of men and the glory of God."[3]

Likewise, Christ calls us, the people of God, by His Word to live holy lives, to shine as lights where we live and work, to do good, so that we will give glory to *our Father* in heaven—doing so in and through Christ, who gives fully sufficient grace for us to live abundantly to the glory of the Father!

Being like your Father in love
In Matthew 5:45 and following, the Sermon continues with the profound and deep application of the law of God to the heart, now focused on love for one's neighbor, particularly one's enemy. Jesus, speaking of loving others in the context of persecution, calls His disciples, the gathered crowds, and us to love our enemies and to pray for those who persecute us! Why? What reason does He give? What motive does He present? The answer is found in Matthew 5:45: "That ye may be the children of your Father which is in heaven."

---

2. Lloyd-Jones, *Sermon on the Mount*, 54.
3. David Dickson, *A Brief Exposition of the Evangel of Jesus Christ According to Matthew* (Edinburgh: Banner of Truth, 1981), 52.

Our Lord is not telling us here that our acts of selfless love are the instrument by which we become sons of the Father. Rather, He is saying that by displaying such love, we demonstrate that we are children of God. By this we show that He is our Father and we are His sons. This is evident because we are striving to be loving—good, gracious, kind, and patient—as He is loving—good, gracious, kind, and patient.

The motivation Christ gives for loving enemies is relational. Charles H. Spurgeon says, "As children we ought to resemble our Father."[4] Have you ever seen this in a child? Perhaps your son has tromped around in your shoes, wanting to be like his daddy? Isn't this true of children who have loving fathers, fathers who show lovingkindness to them even when they are sinful and miserable? Jesus reminds us that God the Father lets His sun shine and His rain fall on the just and the unjust; if we are His children, we should also desire to give without regard for what we receive in return.[5] Jesus is telling us: "Your Father in heaven is so loving, so good, so kind! How patient He is with the wicked, how patient He is with you." Think of John 3:16: "For God so loved the world, that he gave his only begotten Son, that whosoever believeth in him should not perish, but have everlasting life." Be like your Father in heaven, delight in doing what He does, for His glory! Love your neighbor, love your enemies, love those who persecute you!

Your Father's perfection and your motives

Jesus goes on in the following verses to soberly remind us that it is no easy calling He is giving in the Sermon on the Mount. In fact, He says, "Be ye therefore perfect, even as your Father which is in heaven is perfect" (Matt 5:48). Our heavenly Father is perfect in holiness, so He requires perfect holiness. Listen to what our Lord declares in further expounding the call to perfection in relation to the Father in Matthew 6:1–4 and 18: "Take heed that ye do not your alms before men, to be seen of them: otherwise ye have no reward of your Father which is in heaven.... And thy Father which seeth in secret himself

4. Charles H. Spurgeon, *Matthew: The Gospel of the Kingdom* (Pasadena, Tex.: Pilgrim Publications, 1974), 32.

5. Daniel M. Doriani, *Matthew*, Vol. 1 (Phillipsburg, N.J.: Presbyterian and Reformed Publishing, 2008), 191.

will reward thee openly.... [Take heed] that thou appear not unto men to fast, but unto thy Father which is in secret: and thy Father, which seeth in secret, shall reward thee openly."

As Jesus has been declaring in the Sermon on the Mount, the call to complete holiness goes to our hearts, to our motives; it probes to our deepest being. Why do we try to do and be good? Why do we try to follow God's precepts? Is it at root because our hearts are motivated by desire for the praise of men? Or is it because we love the Father and want to glorify Him? God the Father, Jesus tells us, is all-knowing, all-seeing; as our heavenly Father, He is perfectly aware of our motives and situations, and as He observes us from moment to moment, He desires not only that we not be selfishly angry, lustful, deceitful, or vengeful, but also that our outwardly good actions, such as our giving, flow from hearts moved by the desire to glorify Him, to thank Him, and to love Him. This is what our Father desires— holy and good motivation overflowing in holiness and goodness in living; and He promises that He will perfect us in this through sanctification and glorification.[6]

The great encouragement for the Christian is that this call to be perfect, best translated, "Therefore you are to be perfect, as your heavenly Father is perfect" (Matt. 5:48), also contains a promise for the future, closely echoing 1 Peter 1:16, which states, "Be ye holy, for I am holy."[7] Charles Wesley wrote, "He wills that I should holy be: who can withstand his will? The counsel of his grace in me, He surely shall fulfill!"[8]

Communing with your Father in prayer
Nestled within these verses on our heavenly Father's knowledge of our inmost being and His desire for our perfection are our Lord Jesus' instructions on prayer—where the Son again directs our attention to knowing the Father and living in communion with Him. In

6. Doriani, *Matthew*, 194; Lloyd-Jones, *Sermon on the Mount*, 319.

7. In the Greek New Testament, the present imperative is usually expressed by γινομαι; less commonly, as here in Matthew and in 1 Peter, it is expressed by the future of ειμι. The King James Version renders both of these texts beginning with "be ye," transmitting the imperative command but losing the fact that the future also reflects that this command is one given by Christ with promise.

8. Charles Wesley, "I Know That My Redeemer Lives," in *Trinity Hymnal, Revised Edition* (Suwanee, Ga.: Great Commission Publications, 2008), 690.

Matthew 6:6, we read, "Pray to thy Father which is in secret; and thy Father which seeth in secret shall reward thee openly." Jesus reemphasizes here that our lives are open books before the Father, that we live and move and have our being in His presence. He desires our hearts, He desires communion with us—He wants us to speak to Him in prayer, moved by love for Him apart from external motives. The English Puritan Samuel Lee said:

> Secret prayer…is the mark of a sincere heart, and has the promise of a gracious return…. When you are alone in prayer, when it is simply God and you, with this key you open the chambers of Paradise, and enter the closet of divine love…. [The Father's] eye is upon you with a gracious aspect when you are withdrawn from the world…. An invisible God is delighted with invisible prayers, when no eye sees but his; he takes most pleasure in the secret glances of a holy heart.[9]

In Matthew 6:8, our Lord, reflecting on the repetitious prayers of the heathen, tells us, "Be not ye therefore like unto them: for your Father knoweth what things ye have need of, before ye ask him." In his preaching on this passage, Spurgeon states, "God does not need us to pray for his information…nor are we to pray in a mindless repetition," but rather "we pray as children to a Father," a Father who intimately knows and understands us.[10]

Our Father desires us to be holy; He desires that we want to be holy—that first of all privately, and out of that publicly, we display His holiness on earth as it is in heaven. He desires that we pray that His holiness would be magnified everywhere and His will would be done everywhere, including in our own lives.

In verse 9 and following, the Son teaches us further about prayer, communion with the Father:

> After this manner therefore pray ye: Our Father which art in heaven, Hallowed be thy name. Thy kingdom come. Thy will be done in earth, as it is in heaven. Give us this day our daily bread. And forgive us our debts, as we forgive our debtors. And lead

---

9. Samuel Lee, "How to Manage Secret Prayer," in *Puritan Sermons 1659–1689 Being the Morning Exercises at Cripplegate*, Vol. 2 (Wheaton, Ill.: Richard Owen Roberts, Publishers, 1981), 165–67.

10. Spurgeon, *Matthew*, 34.

us not into temptation, but deliver us from evil: For thine is the kingdom, and the power, and the glory, for ever. Amen.

Our Father in heaven desires that we look to Him and trust in Him for our daily provisions in life; for all the grace and forgiveness we need for present and eternal life in His presence; and for the preservation and perseverance we need through the present world of sin. Our Father in heaven desires that we know, and that we tell Him we know, that all is His—the kingdom, the power, and the glory, forever!

Following right on the heels of this call to personal communion in prayer with our heavenly Father (the One who is perfectly holy, and yet full of grace and willingness to forgive), Jesus calls His disciples, then and now, to mirror this holiness and forgiveness, reminding us that this is an essential mark of the child of God! In Matthew 6:14–15, He tells us, "For if ye forgive men their trespasses, your heavenly Father will also forgive you: but if ye forgive not men their trespasses, neither will your Father forgive your trespasses." Our heavenly Father takes keen interest not only in our being forgiven through the work of His Son, but also that we are forgiving—just as He is.

Trusting in your wise and generous Father
A further concentration of references to the Father follows in Matthew 6:26–32 and 7:11. Jesus describes the birds of the air, telling us that our heavenly Father feeds them, and aren't we of more value than they are? In 6:32, after describing the pressures of our human need to obtain food, drink, and clothing, He reminds us that our heavenly Father knows that we need these things. In 7:11, reflecting on prayer with the illustration of a child asking a father for food and receiving what is good, He says "How much more shall your Father which is in heaven give good things to them that ask him?" Jesus tenderly and lovingly points us, and the crowds hearing him, to the Father's great care and love for His people.

Our Father is the One who provides for all of creation, and His children are of far greater value to Him than the birds of the air, which He delights to provide for. Our heavenly Father knows all of our needs; His knowledge is not only the knowledge of perfect holiness, but also the knowledge of perfect care and tender compassion. He, our Father in heaven, is the One who delights to give good things to those who ask Him. How good our Father is! How marvelous that

He would reveal Himself to us by His own Son, coming in the flesh to this sinful world for our salvation! What a mystery is the love of the Father, that His own dear Son would come willingly, sent by Him, to our sin-filled and miserable world to both welcome us into the Father's strong and tender care and make this possible through His own sacrificial work!

Is He Your Father?

A final, distinctive reference to God the Father is made by our Lord Jesus Christ in Matthew 7:21. While Jesus has addressed the gathered disciples and crowds in gracious, covenantal terms, pointing them to God the Father as their Father, pointing us to God the Father as our Father, pointing you to life with God as your Father, He now turns to give us a covenantal warning: "Not every one that saith unto me, Lord, Lord, shall enter into the kingdom of heaven; but he that doeth the will of my Father which is in heaven."

Not all are sons of the Father. In Matthew 7:20, Jesus says we will recognize them by their fruits. All who are children of God are so only by faith in the righteousness of His only begotten Son. Among the gathered disciples at this point, by Luke's account, was Judas Iscariot. We know as well that there were likely those in the crowd who were unconverted—in fact, many abandoned Jesus during the course of His ministry. The Sermon on the Mount as a whole is deeply convicting and heart-probing—an aspect that comes to a climax here, and is followed by the parable of the wise builder and the fool. Lloyd-Jones states:

> [The Sermon] points us to what we can be [only in Christ]…it not only states the demand; it points to the supply, to the source of power. The Lord Jesus Christ died to enable us to live the Sermon on the Mount…. He died that I might now live the Sermon on the Mount. He has made this possible for me. God gives us grace to face the Sermon on the Mount seriously and honestly and prayerfully until we become living examples of it, and exemplifiers of its glorious teaching.[11]

Jesus' final reference to the Father in Matthew 7:21 raises a question: Are you one who desires to do the will of the Father, one who

---

11. Lloyd-Jones, *Sermon on the Mount*, 18–20.

delights to grow in relationship with God the Father through His only begotten Son, Jesus Christ? Are you hearing Christ and doing what He calls you to do, knowing, trusting, glorifying, and communing with the Father as your Father? Are you living in all the goodness, grace, and richness of the children of God? You cannot do it on your own—you need His grace.

The beauty and marvel is that the Preacher of the Sermon on the Mount, the Son who delights to reveal and glorify the Father, is the One sent by the Father so that you can be His son, His daughter. Christ, as the Redeemer Son, is the one who welcomes you to receive grace, forgiveness, and new life as an adopted child of the Father! In John 17, Jesus, praying to the Father, says that eternal life is knowing the only true God and Jesus Himself, whom the Father sent. He goes on to say: "I have glorified thee on the earth.... I have manifested thy name unto the men which thou gavest me.... Now they have known that all things whatsoever thou hast given me are of thee. For I have given unto them the words which thou gavest me; and they have received them...they have believed.... All mine are thine, and thine are mine.... Holy Father, keep [them] through thine own name" (John 17:4–11). See what kind of love the Father has given to us, that we should be called the children of God!

CHAPTER 9

Counseling and the Fatherhood of God

David Murray

*...your heavenly Father knoweth that
ye have need of all these things.*
—Matthew 6:32b

Our theology drives our lives. What we know and understand about God impacts everything we think, say, and do. It especially controls and directs spiritual activities such as preaching and counseling. It's the latter I wish to consider in this chapter by answering this question: How does the fatherhood of God impact our counseling, our personal ministry of the Word to others in need?

We will look at the impact of God's fatherhood on (1) the counselor, (2) the counselee, and (3) specific counseling problems.

Impact on the Counselor

Before we step into a counseling situation, it's vital that we pause to prayerfully reflect on what we are doing. We should seek the face of God before we see the face of a fellow man or woman.

When we look into God's face through Jesus Christ, we are reminded of two truths: (1) I am my Father's child and (2) I am my Father's representative.

I am my Father's child

God is my Father in two ways: by creation and by grace.

In common with the whole human race, *I am a child of God by creation.* Although we deny the universal fatherhood of God as taught by liberal scholars such as Adolf von Harnack, the fact that God is the Creator of everyone means that, in a limited sense, God is the Father of every human being (Acts 17:28).

In counseling, this reminds me of the fundamental unity and equality of the whole human race, and gives me a fellow feeling, a sympathy with my counselees, including those who are unbelievers. Just as the Father makes the sun to shine and the rain to fall on the just and the unjust (Matt. 5:44–45), so, in imitation of my Father, I am to seek the physical and spiritual good of my fellow creatures.

This truth also reminds me that counselor and counselee alike are dependent on the same Father for life, health, strength, and all other physical resources. "In him we live, and move, and have our being" (Acts 17:28).

However, as a Christian, I must go further. I must go beyond the universal fatherhood of God by creation, because, as a believer in Christ, *I am also now a child of God by grace.*

This is especially important to remember when I am counseling fellow believers, fellow sons and daughters of God the Father. It changes my relationship with them from professional to family. I do not go into the interview as a stranger giving professional help to another stranger. I am a brother in the same family as my counselee.

It also helps me to see the counselee and myself as being simultaneously trained by the same Father. God has brought two of His children together to train both of us, to move both of us from weakness to maturity, from ignorance to knowledge. And, of course, as I walk toward the meeting, I am depending on my Father for all spiritual resources, for me and for the success of my counseling.

I am my Father's representative

Just as the preacher is an ambassador for God in the pulpit, so the counselor is in the counseling session. That challenges me to ask several questions:

- What am I communicating to the counselee about God, especially His fatherhood?

- Am I representing God accurately to this person?

- What does this person think about God when he sees and hears me?

- Do I welcome counselees as God the Father would?

- Do I communicate warm empathy or cold indifference?

- Is my body language and appearance "fatherly" or "kingly"?

- Are my words and the spirit in which I speak them fair reflections of the Father?

- Am I getting in the way of the Father or am I helping brothers and sisters toward the Father?

Remembering the fatherhood of God should make counselors more loving, more sympathetic, more dependent, and more God-like.

Impact on the Counselee

Many counseling problems are at least partly caused by ignorance, error, or forgetting about God. Each finds at least part of its answer, and usually a large part, in teaching the counselee about God.

With reference to the fatherhood of God, I want to ask counselees two questions: (1) What do you know about the Father? and (2) Do you know the Father? The first question is an intellectual question regarding facts. The second is an experiential question about faith.

What do you know about the Father?

Often a counselee has very little knowledge or very wrong views of God the Father. I therefore want to inquire into his or her theology. I have found that most errors about God the Father revolve around four misconceptions, which are often related to counselees' experiences of their own fathers.

First, there is the misconception of the Father as *hard*. Often suffering people conclude from their pain that God does not care, or at least not for them: He seems unfeeling, cruel, and vindictive. Or perhaps they have been abused by their fathers—verbally, physically, sexually—and transfer their earthly experience of fatherhood (or of a "father figure") to their heavenly Father.

Second, there is the opposite problem, the misconception of the Father as *indulgent*, which again is often a consequence of counselees' experiences of their fathers. Maybe they were spoiled, or they have seen again and again that most fathers are indulgent with their children. Or perhaps they have swallowed the culture's predominant representation of God as a cuddly cosmic sugar daddy who gives everyone what he or she wants.

Third, there is the classic deist misconception of God as *distant and non-involved*. Again, in an epidemic of absent fathers, this can be a perfectly understandable conclusion.

Fourth, some misconceive of the Father as *sinister*, lurking in the background, hiding in the shadows. The Son is the loving front-figure of the deity, but has to work very hard to keep the malevolent Father "on-board" with the plan of salvation. This is an error that has been around for a long time, an error that Jesus Himself faced down, saying, "He that hath seen me hath seen the Father" (John 14:9). The Father has not hidden or concealed Himself behind Jesus, but has revealed Himself in Jesus.

But, of course, with the "father of lies" continually whispering damaging caricatures of God into sinners' minds, these misconceptions can become deeply engraved on people's hearts, impacting their relationship with God and their response to problems in their lives. A large part of the counseling process usually involves re-educating people about who God is, uncovering lies and replacing them with biblical truth.

When you ask what people know about God the Father, people might not see a clear connection between this question and their problems. It may be worth explaining why you are pursuing this line of inquiry by briefly demonstrating with an example how our understanding of God impacts our moods, words, and actions.

Once the facts are in, it is very likely that a number of areas may have opened up for ministry of the Word in order to replace false views of God with the truth. Remember, Christians need this as well as unbelievers.

Do you know the Father?
This question takes us into the realm of Christian experience, using the word *know* in the biblical sense of "having intimate personal acquaintance with." Our questioning here is not just an intellectual fact-gathering, but also a searching of the true spiritual state of a person—saved or unsaved, the healthy or unhealthy believer.

The most important question here is whether the person savingly knows God the Father in the only way that is possible—through faith in Jesus Christ (John 14:6).

Assuming the answer to this is yes, the major questions really center upon whether the Christian is living out that knowledge in daily life, and especially in dealing with problems. Is there a daily walk with God? Is there a daily consciousness of God as Father? Is there a looking to Him for guidance, wisdom, and strength? Is there a submitting to His discipline? Is there a personal relationship with this person of the Trinity?

Impact on Counseling Problems

Having surveyed the significant role and impact of the fatherhood of God upon the counselor's approach and the counselee's response to problems, let us now look at what specific counseling problems are helped by specific aspects of God's fatherhood. Which fatherly attributes are especially helpful in which situations?

I must make two qualifications to this. First, while the whole Trinity is involved in every counseling solution, we are limiting ourselves to the role of the Father in counseling solutions. Second, while the fatherhood of God is involved in every counseling scenario, I am picking the issues in which God's fatherliness is especially helpful. These include:

Bereavement. When counseling those who have lost loved ones, we are privileged to point people to the Father of all mercies and the God of all comfort (2 Cor. 1:3–4). In the midst of bereavement's emotional tsunami of fear, devastation, and grief, He is the widow's stay and the orphan's shield (Ps. 68:5–6).

Single parenthood. According to the United States Census Bureau, more than a quarter of all American children live in single-parent households, with 23.1 percent of them living with their mothers and only 3.4 percent with their fathers. Four percent of American children live with neither their fathers nor their mothers. What a mission field for the fatherhood of God! What a message we can bring to lonely single parents and their often-lonely children.

Poverty. In a time of high long-term unemployment, we can help people remember that God the Father owns the cattle on a thousand hills (Ps. 50:10). He knows our needs before we ask (Matt. 6:8). He has promised to provide for His children's needs according to His riches in glory by Christ Jesus (Phil. 4:19). Our daily prayer for daily bread is directed to our daily Provider, our Father who is in heaven.

Abuse. Although it may seem counterintuitive to point an abused child to another Father, this is where theology and biblical teaching can serve to show how different the heavenly Father is from all others. He is a perfect loving Father.

Chastisement. When a Christian is being chastised, he or she needs help to understand that it is the loving hand of the Father holding the rod of correction rather than the punishing hand of a judge exacting retribution (Heb. 12:6). That will help sustain the fainting and quell a rebellious spirit.

Assurance. Some Christians lack assurance of their salvation; often, this is the result of failing to apprehend, believe, or understand the loving fatherhood of God. They should be taught to pray for the spirit of adoption by which they can legitimately cry, "Abba, Father" (Rom. 8:15). Sometimes believers need to be taught how to recognize the Spirit that is already within them.

Anxiety. We all know the worry timeline: school, grades, friends, college, marriage, mortgage, school fees, children, children's marriages, health, pension, inheritance. Worry after increasing worry. But at every stage of this all-pervasive worry, our Father enters and says, "Take no [anxious] thought" (see Matt. 6:25).

But He does not just *tell* us to stop being anxious, as if anyone can simply stop that upon command. Through the Son, He reasons and argues us to peace by pointing to the birds and the wild flowers to demonstrate His care for such little things. Jesus asks, "If your Father is like this toward such little things, will He not care even more for you, His child?"

Injustice. As the judge of all the earth, God promises all victims of injustice that He will do right. He will cut down the wicked no matter how high they rise, and He will lift up His oppressed no matter how low they fall (Psalm 37). What a comfort to all victims of crime, especially unpunished crime!

Prodigal children. Christians need to be reminded to show their prodigal sons the same prodigal love that God the Father showed them when they were rebels. What a pattern of unrelenting love and full forgiveness (Luke 15; Ps. 103:13–14)!

Bitterness. On the subject of forgiveness, we can help motivate people to forgive others by calling them to consider their Father's forgiveness of them. In fact, we can show them that our debts will be forgiven by our heavenly Father only if we forgive others their debts to us as well (Matt. 6:14).

Church disputes. Church difficulties turn churches into battlefields or sports fields. The fatherhood of God reminds Christians in dispute that this is not about what army you are fighting for or what team you are on; rather, it's usually about learning to love and live with your brothers and sisters.

Growth/maturity. While counseling is often viewed as problem solving, part of our discipleship counseling should also be about positively helping people to grow and mature as Christians. God is glorified as Father by fruitful Christian lives (John 15:8). Experiencing God's fatherhood is an area in which we can help people to bear fruit.

Parenting. Perhaps it is especially in parenting that the positive truths of God's fatherhood can be used to help parents train children for the Lord (Eph. 6:4).

Conclusion

I hope you can see that God's fatherhood is not an academic subject. It is a practical truth offering wide-ranging help with life's multiple problems. And it is far more effective than the latest Band-Aid of self-help.

CHAPTER 10

The Father's Beautiful Hand of Blessed Chastisement

Burk Parsons

Wherefore seeing we also are compassed about with so great a cloud of witnesses, let us lay aside every weight, and the sin which doth so easily beset us, and let us run with patience the race that is set before us, looking unto Jesus the author and finisher of our faith; who for the joy that was set before him endured the cross, despising the shame, and is set down at the right hand of the throne of God. For consider him that endured such contradiction of sinners against himself, lest ye be wearied and faint in your minds. Ye have not yet resisted unto blood, striving against sin. And ye have forgotten the exhortation which speaketh unto you as unto children, My son, despise not thou the chastening of the Lord, nor faint when thou art rebuked of him: for whom the Lord loveth he chasteneth, and scourgeth every son whom he receiveth. If ye endure chastening, God dealeth with you as with sons; for what son is he whom the father chasteneth not? But if ye be without chastisement, whereof all are partakers, then are ye bastards, and not sons. Furthermore we have had fathers of our flesh which corrected us, and we gave them reverence: shall we not much rather be in subjection unto the Father of spirits, and live? For they verily for a few days chastened us after their own pleasure; but he for our profit, that we might be partakers of his holiness. Now no chastening for the present seemeth to be joyous, but grievous: nevertheless afterward it yieldeth the peaceable fruit of righteousness unto them which are exercised thereby. Wherefore lift up the hands which hang down, and the feeble knees; and make straight paths for your feet, lest that which is lame be turned out of the way; but let it rather be healed.

—Hebrews 12:1–13

I did not grow up in a Christian home, and when I first heard the gospel as a fifteen-year-old, I sensed God's call on my life to serve Him in pastoral ministry. With the same conversion by which He called me to Christ, God caused me to feel an immediate and burning passion to serve Him in whatever way that He called me to serve Him and His people.

In a few years, after studying the theology of the Scriptures, I came into contact with what is called Calvinism. I hated it. I thought it was heretical. I thought it entirely misrepresented Scripture. I thought it made God a tyrant. I fought the doctrines of election and reprobation with every ounce of free will I could muster. I read everything I could get my hands on as I began to do my own study of Scripture to determine truth from error. For more than two years I made my way through the Bible, comparing passage with passage, trying to understand what God's Word taught about these matters.

Finally, I came to two crucial passages in the New Testament. In Romans 8, I encountered the special, inseparable love of God for His people—that which Jonathan Edwards called the complacent, sweet love of God. There I began to understand that God's love for His people is unique. It is a special, saving love that endures. As I studied Romans 8, it was as if all the doctrines of God's sovereignty came to a beautiful high point, showing me how God's special saving love is demonstrated in the lives of His children. Likewise, Hebrews 12 showed me that discipline is a proof of God's fatherly love for His children. I realized, by the grace of God, that the Father's love—demonstrated in His discipline, His fatherly chastisement—was something I could not ignore. I had come to a point of crisis in my life. I either had to deny the infallible authority of the Scriptures altogether or accept these doctrines as biblical and, therefore, true.

So, God used Romans 8 and Hebrews 12 to cause me to realize that we cannot be separated from the love of God in Christ Jesus—that we, the people of God, have a love from God that cannot be taken away. We cannot be snatched from His hand and we cannot jump out of His hand—nor would we ever be able to want to. God has us in the palm of His hand, impressing His love upon us and graciously pressing us and convicting us by the Holy Spirit. The beautiful doctrine of the saving love of God for His people is foundational if we are rightly to understand the doctrines of election and reprobation, and the whole of our salvation, even as we consider the Trinitarian covenant of redemption before the foundation of the world.

The Example of the Father's Chastisement

In Hebrews 12, the author writes, "For consider him that endured such contradiction of sinners against himself" (v. 3a). The author here is pointing to Christ. He says, "Consider Him, look to Him, fix your eyes on this One." It is no little matter that when Jesus Christ, the Son of God, took on flesh and dwelt among us, that we, in our natural, rebellious state of sin, put Him to death. We may think that we are above that and that we would not have done such to the Lord Jesus Christ, but we need to be reminded that if He came back today, and we were still in our natural, sinful state of enmity against God, we would put Him to death. That's exactly what we did as sinners in our natural state—we put the Lord Jesus Christ to death. No greater contradiction has ever taken place—that Jesus Christ, the Lord of glory, was murdered at the hands of sinners.

Consider this One, the author writes to the Hebrews (and God writes to us now), who "endured the cross, despising the shame" (v. 2), "lest ye be wearied and faint in your minds" (v. 3b). Pressures, afflictions, and trials come against us not only from this world and the devil, but from our own deceitful hearts, which shoot darts and arrows at us from within. We are afflicted by doubts, conflicts, anxieties, and burdens that weigh us down—concerns not only for our own lives and souls but also for loved ones. And if our eyes are open to the wretched sinfulness of this world, nearly every time we drive down the street or watch a news report, we can scarcely avoid being brought to tears, for we see sin, sadness, and misery all around us.

So when we come to this passage, we come, as Alexander Maclaren said, as to a lighthouse. Of course, a lighthouse is not something that we look to in the daytime or when all is going well. If we come to a passage like this when all seems well and the sun is shining brightly, ignoring the realities of sin and sadness, then we are prone to ignore it. We are prone to say: "We'll save that for a darker hour. Let us rejoice in the goodness, happiness, and joys of everything that we are experiencing today, for all is well." We don't want to think about the difficulties, afflictions, and problems of our loved ones, our children, or our grandchildren who may not know the Lord, of those friends next door who are dying and going to hell, of the pains and horrors that many are experiencing throughout the world. It is only when we see the sins of this world and the sins of our own hearts that we see our great need for the lighthouse that God has given us for the darkness. It is always there, and we have only to look to it—not only in the significant times of stresses and anxieties, but every day, every hour, and every minute of our lives, for we need Him every hour. We must understand that God our Father is not only with us in afflictions and trials, He is the author of them, working in us both to will and to do according to His good pleasure. So the author of Hebrews says, "Don't be weary, don't faint in your minds," for that is our tendency.

He continues in verse 4, "Ye have not yet resisted unto blood, striving against sin." The point is very simple: The Hebrews are still alive. They are still breathing. Their hearts are still pumping. They have not yet been killed as the Lord Jesus Christ was killed. Their blood has not yet been spilled in striving against sin. The original recipients of this letter needed to continue to be encouraged to persevere in mortifying sin in the flesh, just as we need to persevere as we delightfully bear fruit of righteousness and pursue holiness by the sustaining grace of God.

The Means of the Father's Chastisement

We then read, "And ye have forgotten the exhortation which speaketh unto you as unto children" (v. 5a). We are apt to forget the promises and truths of God. We are quick to forget what He has taught us— not only by experience and the wisdom He has shown us by His Spirit over our years as Christians, but from His Word. One Sunday we will hear a sermon that revolutionizes our way of thinking and living, and a day later, even hours later, we will forget it entirely. If we would feast throughout the week on the sermons we hear each Lord's Day, daily reflecting on and living out the glorious exhortations and promises proclaimed to us, we would find ourselves bearing daily, even hourly, fruit of repentance unto righteousness. For indeed, the exhortations from God's Word are graciously given to us as the first step of discipline and our training in the fear and admonition of the Lord. Thus, we could rightly deduce that everyone who is a Christian, hearing the exhortations and promises of God, is under the discipline of the church where he is a member. We are under church discipline because we are under the exhortation and training of the Word of God.

Pastors, first and foremost, exist to pray for God's people and to feed God's people with God's Word. Pastors are not primarily called to make people feel good about themselves week in and week out, but to give people the Word of God, in order that we might come away feeling repentant and glorying in Christ, our only hope. I have heard Dr. W. Robert Godfrey say that he does not feel that he has been to church unless he feels a little beaten up afterward. We leave beaten up, on our knees in repentance, but nevertheless rejoicing at having been brought to Jesus Christ through the reviving and consoling gospel.

So, each Lord's Day, having examined ourselves and our hearts, we come to receive the exhortation and gracious discipline that comes from the Word of God, which always drives us to our need for the work of Christ. Is it not a delightful thing that we as the people of God come through the doors of our sanctuary saying, "I need to receive discipline, I need to be reminded of my sin, and I need, most desperately, to be reminded of the grace of God in Jesus Christ"?

Verse 5 goes on, as the author quotes from the books of Proverbs and Job: "My son, despise not thou the chastening of the Lord, nor faint when thou art rebuked of him." We often respond to discipline by despising it. We grow bitter and angry against God, thinking that He not only has turned His face from us, but that He is holding us at arm's length. In fact, when God is disciplining us, He is not far from us at all—His hand is not extended out against us; rather, He has brought us close to Him. He has brought us right up to Himself; He has us in His arms. As He brings His loving hand of chastisement upon us, it is as if He is saying to us, "I am doing this for your good and, ultimately, for My glory, for the sake of My name."

Is that not the reason we discipline our own children? We do it not only for their good but also for our name. When we discipline our children, we are concerned not only that they be instructed rightly so that they are obedient and behave as our Lord instructs, but that they might rightly represent the name of Christ, and, secondly, that they rightly represent their family. When we exhort and discipline our children, we speak to them the truth in love, for discipline is not like the work of an emergency-room doctor, stitching us up as quickly as he possibly can, hurriedly bandaging our wounds. Discipline is more like the work of a surgeon. He has taken the necessary

X-rays and MRIs, he has studied the injury, and he has carefully considered the appropriate remedies, so that, when he begins to cut and perform his surgery, he can hope for proper healing and restoration. So we do with our children, and so God does with His children.

The author of Hebrews also says that this chastening of the Lord is not to make us faint; that is, it is not to make us despise it, grow bitter, or lose heart. We are not to become complacent or cynical toward our heavenly Father's discipline. When discipline comes, our tendency is to keep a stiff upper lip—to act as if nothing is happening. But the purpose of our Father's discipline is to bring us to our knees and that all around us would see our utter need for our Father, that we are wholly dependent on our sovereign God, who disciplines and restores, who gives and who takes away.

The Grace of the Father's Chastisement
In Job 5, we see how the Lord uses Eliphaz the Temanite to teach us about His sovereign ways (although Eliphaz applies them inappropriately to Job's situation). We read:

> Behold, happy is the man whom God correcteth: therefore despise not thou the chastening of the Almighty: for he maketh sore, and bindeth up: he woundeth, and his hands make whole. He shall deliver thee in six troubles: yea, in seven there shall no evil touch thee. In famine he shall redeem thee from death: and in war from the power of the sword. Thou shalt be hid from the scourge of the tongue: neither shalt thou be afraid of destruction when it cometh. At destruction and famine thou shalt laugh: neither shalt thou be afraid of the beasts of the earth. For thou shalt be in league with the stones of the field: and the beasts of the field shall be at peace with thee. And thou shalt know that thy tabernacle shall be in peace; and thou shalt visit thy habitation, and shalt not sin. Thou shalt know also that thy seed shall be great, and thine offspring as the grass of the earth. Thou shalt come to thy grave in a full age, like as a shock of corn cometh in in his season. Lo this, we have searched it, so it is; hear it, and know thou it for thy good (vv. 17–27).

Let me draw your attention especially to the first words of this passage: "Behold, happy is the man whom God correcteth: therefore despise not thou the chastening of the Almighty: for he maketh sore, and bindeth up: he woundeth, and his hands make whole." The sores, the shattering, and the breaking of our bones are all authored by our sovereign Lord. As our Chief Shepherd, He goes out into the field and disciplines us as He brings us to repentance by breaking us of our seemingly self-sufficient strength, breaking our knees as it were that we might get down to feed in the green pasture of His Word. Then, as He restores our souls, He keeps our enemies at bay that we might feast, and He takes us by the hand and leads us beside waters that He has stilled so that we can drink freely and enjoy an abundant life under the shadow of our almighty Shepherd.

Is it not our prayer that God would shatter us? That God would make us sore? That God would bring us to the end of ourselves that we might find Him? Is this not your prayer for those you most love? You worry that your children, grandchildren, friends, brothers, sisters, or even spouses may not really know the Lord Jesus Christ. You worry that they might be among those to whom Jesus will say on the last day, "I never knew you: depart from me, ye that work iniquity" (Matt. 7:23). Do we not pray that God would break them down and bring them to the end of themselves? That God would bring them, through His loving chastisement, to Himself?

If you have never experienced the chastisement of God, you may not be a Christian. But if you are among the elect of God, you will, by His grace, experience it, and He will, by His grace, bring you to the end of yourself. So, as we grow in grace and holiness, we will increasingly pray, "Loving Father, bring Thy loving chastisement upon me, and by Thy goodness lead me to repentance." Furthermore, we will also pray for God's loving discipline of our families and even for the discipline of our neighbors. One of the greatest ways we can pray for the impenitent is to ask, "Lord, if they are Thy elect children, then bring them to the end of themselves and to their knees before Jesus Christ."

My father died at the age of sixty-eight in 1992. I was sixteen years old. Many of us have lost parents, and if you lost a father or mother when you were young, you miss not only their companionship, not only the opportunity to speak to them, but the opportunity to listen to them, to hear even their words of exhortation. What I missed most about my father, as I grew as a teenager and then entered college and seminary, was having someone to admonish me, someone whom I respected who would exhort me. From time to time when I received a word of exhortation from my father, he would say, "You are my beloved son, in whom I am well-pleased." I did not know what those words meant, I did not know their import, and I had no idea where they came from, but I delighted in them. This is what we long for, is it not? We long for fathers who care enough about us to exhort us in love.

The Hope of the Father's Chastisement

The author of Hebrews continues, "If ye endure chastening, God dealeth with you as with sons" (v. 7a). If we endure discipline, not fainting under it or losing heart, the certain hope is that "God dealeth with you as with sons." If we endure it as the Spirit sustains us, and as our Father grants the faith to persevere, we are proven to be children of God.

Several years ago, I had the opportunity to edit a book on the Christian's assurance of salvation called *Assured by God*. I asked Jerry Bridges to write a chapter for that book on a subject that I knew I could likely not handle well as a young pastor. The chapter is titled, "The Blessing of Discipline." Some readers asked, "Why include a chapter on discipline in a book on assurance?" It seemed contradictory to them, but I believe God's promise to chastise His children is one of the most practical and observable assurances that we are in Christ. We can rest assured that we belong to God when His hand of discipline comes upon us so as to sanctify us. It demonstrates that God loves us. It shows us that we will never be separated from Him. It shows us that we are His eternal children.

The author writes, "If ye endure chastening, God dealeth with you as with sons; for what son is he whom the father chasteneth not? But if ye be without chastisement, whereof all are partakers, then are ye bastards, and not sons" (vv. 7–8). That's significant language: "bastards" are illegitimate sons. Yes, illegitimate children have parents, but the author of Hebrews is making the simple point that if we do not receive God's chastisement, we are not *His* children. Not only that, but as Jesus said, "Ye are of your father the devil" (John 8:44). If we do not receive chastisement, we have no Father who will give us eternal life.

He goes on to say, "Furthermore we have had fathers of our flesh which corrected us, and we gave them reverence: shall we not much rather be in subjection unto the Father of spirits, and live?" (v. 9). Jesus uses similar language and paints a similar scenario in Matthew 7: "Or what man is there of you, whom if his son ask bread, will he give him a stone? Or if he ask a fish, will he give him a serpent? If ye then, being evil, know how to give good gifts unto your children, how much more shall your Father which is in heaven give good things to them that ask him?" (vv. 9–11). Our Father is ready to give us bread, but often we simply ask for stones, and even expect them. Our Father is giving us bread, but He often gives it through the afflictions that bring us to the point of knowing how much we need the bread. He leads us through the wilderness at times, so that when we feed on that which He provides us, we are grateful to have that which only the hand of God can provide, the only bread that can truly and eternally satisfy.

The Goal of the Father's Chastisement
We then read, "For they verily for a few days chastened us after their own pleasure" (v. 10a). Our earthly fathers chastened us after their own wisdom, "but he for our profit, that we might be partakers of his holiness" (v. 10b). The goal of discipline is not simply that we might have better lives. It is that we would share in God's holiness. God raises us up to make us mature. He gives us the character and the hope that does not disappoint, because of the love that He has poured out in our hearts by His Spirit. God makes us complete and mature, lacking nothing. The goal is that we would become more and more dependent on Christ, fixing our eyes on Him and thus becoming more like Him in His holiness.

That's why, at the outset of chapter 12, the author of Hebrews draws us to Christ Himself: "Wherefore seeing we also are compassed about with so great a cloud of witnesses, let us lay aside every weight, and the sin which doth so easily beset us, and let us run with patience the race that is set before us, looking unto Jesus the author and finisher of our faith; who for the joy that was set before him endured the cross, despising the shame, and is set down at the right hand of the throne of God" (vv. 1–2). We are not in an arbitrary race; it is an "authored" race. Our race has been sovereignly established by God. There is a finish line that, by His grace, if we are His children, we will cross victoriously in Christ as we cross it behind Him. He leads from the beginning. He is not only our Elder Brother in the faith who went before us and gained the victory, but the One who authored our race and our faith. He is the One who leads us out onto the racetrack and the battlefield of this life. He is not standing behind us, telling us to run and fight the battle, but He is charging the enemy, going in front of us that we might see Him at all times at the forefront. So, in coming behind Him, we are not looking at our swords and the strength of our weaponry, and neither are we trusting in our horses and chariots. We are not looking down at the problems and the weakness of our own manufactured earthly weaponry, for in doing so, we would trip and lose the battle; our striving would be losing. Instead, we are looking at our Captain. We are looking at the One who goes forth conquering and to conquer, vanquishing all His and our enemies.

Christ is at the forefront of the battle, and we are called to fix our eyes on Him. No matter what enemies come our way, no matter how our weapons fail us, no matter how we are attacked, may our eyes remain fixed on Jesus Christ, the Author and the Finisher of our faith, the One who goes before us and wins the battle over the world, the flesh, and the devil. When He says to His disciples in the upper room, "Be of good cheer; I have overcome the world" (John 16:33b), we know that our victory is in the Victor, Jesus Christ, and can rest assured that anything that comes our way is all for our good and His glory, that we might share in His holiness.

In Christ, we not only bear "the peaceable fruit of righteousness" (v. 11), but a full and abundant harvest of fruit from a vast field of blessing. That fruit comes forth by the disciplining hand of God, weaning us from the world, rooting out sin, mortifying our flesh, and making us not only have no taste for the things of this world and our own flesh, but making us actually hate it. Is not this our greatest prayer: "Lord, help me to hate sin as Thou dost hate sin. May I have a love for Thee that bypasses all other loves in my life. May I have the kind of peace that is associated with that love, as I will in the new heaven and new earth." Is not one of our greatest joys the knowledge that we will be free from sin and even free from the possibility of being able to sin? Is not one of our greatest hopes that we will be surrounded by those who cannot sin against us, and even more, that we will no longer be able to sin against the God we love?

This is what He is preparing us for even now. He disciplines us through conviction by His Spirit, by pricking our consciences and saying: "See your sin for what it is. Resist it. Be willing to do whatever is appropriate and necessary while you still have breath, and do not faint or grow weary in doing good. Do not grow bitter. Do not grow complacent or cynical. Stay the course and finish the race, for Christ has overcome the world."

The Father's hand of discipline will feel heavy but will appear beautiful to His children. For we who are God's come daily like little children and fall upon our knees in faith, resting upon Christ alone for salvation as He is offered to us in the gospel, knowing that the Son of God was wounded for our transgressions and bruised for our iniquities, and that the chastisement of our peace was upon Him, and with His stripes we are healed.

CONCLUSION

CHAPTER 11

The Need for a
Trinitarian Piety

Ryan McGraw

*For through him we both have access
by one Spirit unto the Father.*
—Ephesians 2:18

The Savoy Declaration of Faith and Order (1658) asserts that the "doc-trine of the Trinity is the foundation of all our communion with God, and comfortable dependence upon him."[1] The Dutch theologian Gisbertus Voetius (1589–1676) referred to the Trinity as the founda-tion of fundamentals (*fundamentum fundamenti*), and he added that every article of the faith is married to this doctrine.[2] Today, however, many believers have little or no practical use for God's triunity in their everyday lives. In the early eighteenth century, the doctrine of the Trinity fell into decline. While some in the church fought for the doctrine for decades, those finely tuned doctrinal disputes gradually lost touch with the faith and lives of ordinary believers. Eventually, some in the church began to wonder what all of the fuss was about. This led many churches to become Unitarian.[3]

---

1. Savoy Declaration, 2.3.
2. Gisperti Voetii, *Selectarum Disputationum Theologicarum, Pars Prima* (Utrecht: 1648), 1:472, 478.
3. Philip Dixon relates that in the early eighteenth century, Church of England theologian Daniel Waterland (1683–1740) made one of the last attempts to show the practical importance of the Trinity. This attempt illustrates the general decline of the doctrine. Dixon notes, "Instead of a sense of the centrality of the doctrine to the whole of Christian experience, the reader is left with the feeling that Waterland is desperately trying to make the doctrine of the Trinity 'relevant.'" He concludes, "The doctrine of the Trinity remained the official teaching of the Church of England but had little impact on its life." Philip Dixon, *Nice and Hot Disputes: The Doctrine of the Trinity in the Seventeenth Century* (London: T&T Clark, 2003), 205–7.

Is our generation on the verge of falling into the same kind of apostasy? Have you ever wondered why the Trinity is so essential to the Christian faith? We know the persons of the Godhead better by experiencing their saving work in our lives than we do by man-made analogies.[4] Even if we can define this doctrine biblically,[5] if the triunity of God does not stand at the heart of our Christianity, then the doctrine remains in danger. Biblical truth that is not practical or experimental is a kind of half-truth only.[6] The Trinity is no exception to this rule.[7]

This book is the fruit of the third of three conferences on the beauty and the glory of each person of the Godhead. This chapter aims to tie together the themes of these three conferences by demonstrating why we must self-consciously think of the gospel in terms of the work of all three divine persons. Paul's statement in Ephesians 2:18 highlights this need well. This passage teaches us that communion with all three persons of the Godhead is essential for the piety[8] and growth in grace of the church. In light of this text, we will consider the importance of the doctrine of the Trinity, the structure of a Trinitarian piety, and the application of Trinitarian piety.

The Importance of the Doctrine of the Trinity

Cults frequently ask us to prove the doctrine of the Trinity from Scripture.[9] However, perhaps the greatest "proof" of the triunity of God is that Christ and His apostles never proved the doctrine directly. Instead, the Trinity is the backdrop of the entire New Testament and its teaching.[10] Whether we look at the baptism of Christ (Matt. 3:13–17),

---

4. Johannes Hoornbeeck (1617–1666), *Theologiae Practicae* (Utrecht, 1663), 1:136.

5. For a concise definition of the doctrine of the Trinity, see the Westminster Shorter Catechism, Q. 6: "There are three persons in the Godhead, the Father, the Son, and the Holy Ghost, and these three are one God, the same in substance, equal in power and glory."

6. Hoornbeeck, *Theologiae Practicae*, 1:5.

7. See Voetii, *Disputationum Theologicarum*, 1:478.

8. *Piety* is often misunderstood as a term. I am largely using it here as a synonym for personal holiness. See Richard A. Muller, *Dictionary of Latin and Greek Theological Terms* (Grand Rapids: Baker, 1985), 228.

9. Mormons and Jehovah's Witnesses among others.

10. "Understanding [of the doctrine of the Trinity] unfolds from the Christian experience of salvation; conceptualization follows later. The expression of the Trinity is rooted in personal salvation and Christian experience, not abstract

the baptism of believers (Matt. 28:19), the work of redemption (1 Peter 3:18; Heb. 9:28), God's eternal plan (Eph. 1:3–14), the doctrine of the church (Eph. 4:1–10), or God's blessing upon His people (2 Cor. 13:14), the authors of the New Testament consistently described Christian doctrine and living by presupposing the unity of the Godhead and the distinct persons of the Father, the Son, and the Holy Spirit. If the thread of the triunity of God were removed, the garment of Scripture and especially of the New Testament would unravel.[11]

Ephesians 2:18 ("For through him we both have access by one Spirit unto the Father") is a vivid example of the Trinitarian presupposition behind the gospel. This passage is well-suited to highlight the need for a self-consciously Trinitarian faith and piety.[12] Ephesians 2:11–22 describes the nature of peace between God and mankind, as well as between believers. All humanity had been divided previously into Jews and Gentiles (i.e., everyone who was not a Jew). Now, in Christ, the Gentiles who were once strangers from the covenant promises of God and from the society of His people have been brought near through faith in Christ (vv. 11–13). Verses 14–18 describe how this twofold reconciliation between God and men and between Jews and Gentiles is possible. Verse 14 serves as a grand title to the entire section: "For he is our peace."[13] Peace between God and man and peace among men is not so much a gift as it is a person. Christ is the Prince of Peace (Isa. 9:6); there is no true and lasting peace with God or with others apart from union and communion with Him. Our great Redeemer has removed the condemning power of the law (vv. 15–16). When we rest in the person and work of Christ through faith alone, we are "in Christ" (Eph. 1:1–6). Just as American citizens are safe and protected from foreign powers when they stand on

---

speculation." Robert Letham, *The Holy Trinity: In Scripture, History, Theology, and Worship* (Phillipsburg, N.J.: P&R Publishing, 2004), 68.

11. For a sober and careful examination of the Trinity in the Old Testament, see Letham, *The Holy Trinity*, 17–33. The most extensive Reformed treatment of the doctrine of the Trinity in the Old Testament remains Jerome Zanchi (1516–1590), *De Tribus Elohim, Aeterno Patre, Filio, et Spirito Sancto, Uno Eodemque Iohova, Librie XIII, in Duas Distincti Partes* (Nestadii Palatinorum, 1597). This work was cited by virtually all Reformed authors who wrote on the Trinity in the seventeenth century.

12. John Owen (1616–1683) would have agreed. He cited Ephesians 2:18 frequently in his printed works.

13. Peter T. O'Brien, *The Letter to the Ephesians* (Grand Rapids: Eerdmans, 1999), 193.

American soil, so believers are safe "in Christ," who defends them against all the assaults of sin, death, and hell.

Verse 18 is the centerpiece of Paul's argument in this paragraph.[14] This makes his allusion to all three persons of the Godhead all the more significant. As D. Martyn Lloyd-Jones (1899–1981) wrote, "Here is one of the great Trinitarian verses of Scripture, and we pause for a moment before its ineffable mystery."[15] Christ is here the great and central means through which sinners come to God ("through him"). The Spirit is the divine person by whose work we come to the Father through Christ ("by one Spirit"). "*One* Spirit" stresses the unity of the church (see 1 Cor. 12:1ff). Since all believers participate in the saving work of the Spirit of God, they are one with God and one with each other. Finally, the Father is the goal, or the destination, toward which believers go through the Son and by the Spirit ("to the Father"). When we unpack this language, a divine order emerges clearly. As Christians, we come by (*en*) the Spirit, through (*dia*) the Son, to (*pros*) the Father.[16] In Ephesians 1:3–14, Paul conversely described God approaching us in salvation from the Father, through the Son, by the Spirit. This means that two-way traffic between God and His creatures follows this specific Trinitarian order.[17] It is impossible to have communion with one person in the Godhead without having communion with all three persons.[18] It is also impossible to come

---

14. O'Brien, *Ephesians*, 208; F. F. Bruce, *The Epistles to the Colossians, to Philemon, and to the Ephesians* (Grand Rapids: Eerdmans, 1984), 301.

15. D. Martyn Lloyd-Jones, *God's Way of Reconciliation: An Exposition of Ephesians 2* (Grand Rapids: Baker, 1998), 246. Interestingly, very few Bible commentators show in practice that they agree with Lloyd-Jones. Most of them, including O'Brien and Bruce, make passing reference to the Trinity here as though it does not lie at the crux of Paul's reasoning.

16. Hoornbeeck provides a careful treatment of the terms used to describe the interrelation of the divine persons in the work of salvation. Hoornbeeck, *Theologiae Practicae*, 1:136–37.

17. For expansion on this point, see Peter Toon, *Our Triune God: A Biblical Portrayal of the Trinity* (Vancouver: Regent College Publishing, 2002), 213–29.

18. In theological terms, this fact has often been described in terms of the mutual indwelling of the persons (*perichoresis*) and the resultant idea that the works of the Godhead are always the undivided work of all three persons (*opera trinitatis ad extra indivisa sunt*). The work of each person is distinct in terms of emphasis, but all three persons always act in the same work at the same time. See J. van Genderen and W. H. Velema, *Concise Reformed Dogmatics* (Phillipsburg, N.J.: P&R Publishing, 2008), 153–54, 158–60.

to the Father without coming to Him through the Son and by the Holy Spirit. No one comes to the Father apart from Christ (John 14:6). Moreover, the Spirit convinces the world of sin, righteousness, and judgment, in order to drive sinners to Christ (John 16:8–11). Thus, the triune God is the basis for the apostle Paul's teaching on the peace and unity of the church. Before we can have peace with others, we must have peace with God, through Christ, by the Spirit.

Has Christ become your peace? Do you rest upon Him as the only means by which you can come to the Father? Do you recognize that you cannot embrace Christ or come to the Father through Him without the Spirit's work in your heart? Do you understand your helplessness on account of your sin? Have you come to recognize that unless you are born from above, you cannot see the kingdom of God (John 3:3)?

This truth should dispel some of the delusional attempts that some have made toward a broad trans-denominational union.[19] Genuine unity among Christians is rooted in the unified work of the persons of the Godhead. How can we be one with each other unless we are first one with God, through Christ, by the Spirit? Like Paul, we must place the work of the triune God at the heart of the gospel, as well as at the center of our own personal holiness, before we can discuss any true basis of Christian unity.

The Structure of a Trinitarian Piety

In order to better understand how to weave the Trinity into our faith and piety, it is vital to unpack the particular work of each divine person in our salvation. Many people are familiar with John Bunyan's (1628–1688) classic work *The Pilgrim's Progress*, in which Christian makes his way to the gates of the Celestial City. However, fewer people know that Bunyan wrote a sequel to this work. In part two, Christian's wife, Christiana, is converted to Christ. She and her children then begin to follow the path that their husband and father trod before them. At one point in the journey, a character named Prudence asks Christiana's youngest son three questions regarding how each person in the Godhead is his Savior. We are used to thinking

---

19. For a helpful evaluation of false attempts at Christian unity in the twentieth century, see Iain H. Murray, *Evangelicalism Divided: A Record of Crucial Change in the Years 1950 to 2000* (Edinburgh: Banner of Truth Trust, 2000).

of Christ as the Savior; few of us give thought to the work of the Father and the Spirit in salvation. Could we answer these questions as Christiana's young child could?[20] The way in which the work of the Father, the Son, and the Holy Spirit lays the foundation for our faith determines how each person shapes our personal holiness.

The Father

Paul laid his stress upon coming to the Father.[21] Christ placed the same emphasis in the Lord's Prayer. While Stephen prayed to Christ when he was stoned to death ("Lord Jesus, receive my spirit," Acts 7:59), and while we may pray to any or all three divine persons, calling upon the Father is the ordinary pattern for our prayers (Matt. 6:9; 1 Peter 1:17).[22] Calling God our Father is our highest privilege.

Adoption is often presented as a summary of all of the benefits of the gospel (Gal. 4:4–6; John 1:12).[23] Jesus addressed God as "Father" (Mark 14:36). The Holy Spirit teaches believers to address God as He did (Rom. 8:15; Gal. 4:6). Because Christ is the natural Son of God, those who are united to Him by faith are adopted sons of God (Eph. 1:5). When we are tempted to regard Christ as a gentle and welcoming Savior, but to think of the Father as a distant and austere Judge, we do well to remember who so loved the world that He gave His only begotten Son to die for His people (John 3:16; Matt. 1:21). The

---

20. John Bunyan, *The Pilgrim's Progress From This World to That Which Is To Come, The Second Part* (London, 1687), 76–77. Prudence then tells Christiana: "You are to be commended for thus bringing up your children. I suppose I need not ask the rest these questions, since the youngest of them can answer them so well" (77).

21. John Owen wrote in *Communion with God,* in *The Works of John Owen* (reprint, Edinburgh: Banner of Truth, 1968), 2:17, 19, "This is the great *discovery* of the gospel: for whereas the Father, as the fountain of the Deity, is not known any other way than as full of wrath, anger, and indignation against sin, nor can the sons of men have any other thoughts of him (Rom. i. 18; Is. xxxiii. 13,14; Hab. i. 13; Ps. v. 4–6; Eph. ii. 3),—here he is now revealed peculiarly as love, as full of it unto us; the manifestation whereof is the peculiar work of the gospel, Titus iii. 4." See Lloyd-Jones, *God's Way of Reconciliation*, 250.

22. See Henry Scudder (1585–1653), *A Key of Heaven: The Lord's Prayer Opened and so Applied, that a Christian May Learn How to Pray, and to Procure all Things which May Make for the Glory of God, and the Good of Himself and of His Neighbor; Containing Likewise such Doctrines of Faith and Godliness, as May be Very Useful to All that Desire to Live Godly in Christ Jesus* (London, 1633), 89–90.

23. B. M. Palmer writes, "Adoption is possibly the most comprehensive of our evangelical terms. All the doctrines of grace are folded within it, and emerge in its analysis." *A Theology of Prayer* (Harrisonburg, Va.: Sprinkle Publications, 1980), 208.

Father's electing love and purpose stand behind the entire gospel. Christ is like a mirror in which we behold the Father's love.[24]

Apart from Christ, we cannot be assured of the Father's love, but in Christ, how can we doubt the Father's love? The love of the Father should drive us to pursue personal holiness out of gratitude toward Him and respect for His fatherly authority. If the Father has so loved us, then should we not respond to Him in kind? We must love the Father with our hearts, minds, souls, and strength. The Father's love is our primary motive for personal holiness.

The Son
The person and work of Jesus Christ form the centerpiece of the gospel. He is like a great jewel set prominently in the midst of a spectacular treasure room. While the entire room full of riches is blinding in its brilliance, the jewel on display at the heart of the room immediately attracts the attention of all who enter. So is Christ in relation to God's plan of salvation.

It has become common to say that we must have a personal relationship with Jesus Christ if we desire to be saved. This statement is as undoubtedly true as it is insufficient. Believers enjoy a personal relationship with Christ because they are in union with Christ. Union includes a personal relationship with Him, but it is much more than that.[25]

Union with Christ is easier to experience than it is to define.[26] It is comparable to the difference between marriage and friendship. As closely as a man and a woman may walk together in fellowship as friends, this relationship differs radically from the union that exists between a husband and wife. This is the only earthly relationship that comes close to describing the union between Christ and His church (Eph. 5:32). Yet even marital union pales in comparison to the union between Christ and His bride. Union with Christ means that His obedience is my obedience (Rom. 5:19), that His righteousness is

---

24. This illustration is adapted from John Calvin, *Institutes of the Christian Religion*, ed. John T. McNeill, trans. Ford Lewis Battles (Philadelphia: Westminster Press, 1960), 3.24.5.

25. See Thomas Manton (1620–1677), *The Works of Thomas Manton* (Birmingham, Ala.: Solid Ground Christian Books, 2010), 11:27.

26. See Robert Letham, *Union with Christ: In Scripture, History, and Theology* (Phillipsburg, N.J.: P&R Publishing, 2011), 1.

my righteousness (2 Cor. 5:21), that His death removed my curse and the wrath of God from me (Gal. 3:13), that His resurrection results in my personal holiness and in the resurrection of my body (Rom. 6:1ff; 1 Cor. 15:12ff), and that His ascension secures my place in heaven (Phil. 3:20; John 14:1–2). Even these statements barely scratch the surface of what union with Christ means.

This is why Paul says that we come to the Father, through Christ, by one Spirit. He made the person and work of Christ the central focus of the saving work of God in all divine-human relationships.[27] Christ is the basis of our relation to God as well as to other believers. In Christ, we have everything necessary to give us right standing before God. In Christ, we have everything necessary for life and for godliness (2 Peter 1:3). The grace of Jesus Christ is the foundation or ground of our personal holiness.

The Holy Spirit

The Holy Spirit is the bond of our union and fellowship with the Father and the Son. He applies Christ to our hearts through the Word. He is the down payment of our inheritance in heaven and He is the seal of our adoption (2 Cor. 1:22; 5:5). We confess that Jesus is Lord through Him and because of Him (1 Cor. 12:3). In terms of our status before God in Christ, He unites us to Jesus Christ by working faith in us (1 Cor. 2:12–16; see also Phil. 1:29; Eph. 3:17). He is the author of our prayers (Rom. 8:26; Eph. 6:18; Jude 20) and of every godly yearning of our hearts. We pray to the Father, in the name of Christ, by the help of the Spirit.[28] In short, the Holy Spirit is the cause of saving union with Christ as well as of all personal holiness through fellowship with the Godhead. He uses the public means of grace to draw

---

27. James Durham (1622–1658) gave eight reasons why true Trinitarianism should always lead to a Christ-centered emphasis. Durham, *A Commentarie upon the Book of Revelation, Wherein the Text is Explained, the Series of Several Prophecies Contained in that Book, Deduced and According to their Order and Dependence upon Each Other; the Periods and Succession of Times, at, or About Which, these Prophecies, that are Already Fulfilled, Began to be, and Were More Fully Accomplished, Fixed and Applied According to History, and Those that are yet to be Fulfilled, Modestly, and so far as it is Warrantable, Enquired into; Together with Some Practical Observations, and Several Digressions, Necessary for Vindicating, Clearing, and Confirming Many Weighty and Important Truths* (Edinburgh, 1658), 12–14.

28. Scudder, *A Key of Heaven*, 41.

us near to God, especially the Word, the sacraments, and prayer.[29] In this sense, the Holy Spirit is the immediate cause of all personal holiness, religious affections, and communion with God.

Putting the picture together
All three persons of the Godhead save us. The distinct and united work of the Father, the Son, and the Spirit is the foundation of our relation to God as well as of our relation to others. This is why we must be self-consciously Trinitarian in our piety and in our personal godliness. We must walk by faith and not by sight (2 Cor. 5:7). The Trinity is not only the central and foundational doctrine of the gospel, but the foundation of every aspect of the Christian life. As we began our Christian lives on the basis of the work of all three persons, so we must continue to walk with God on the same basis. To the degree that we are not self-consciously Trinitarian in our piety, we impoverish our Christian experience as well as our growth in grace and in holiness.

Do you rest daily upon the grace of the Lord Jesus Christ, the love of God, and the fellowship of the Holy Spirit (2 Cor. 13:14)? Do you worship the Father, in the Holy Spirit, and through Christ who is the truth (John 4:21–24)? If you would do these things, then you must begin acquainting yourself with the work of each divine person in your salvation. This is why Paul made the triune God Himself the foundation of peace and unity in the church.

The Application of a Trinitarian Piety
Many theologians have taught that we cannot understand a doctrine truly unless we know it in our personal experience and practice.[30] As Edward Reynolds (1599–1676), wrote: "Christ is not truly apprehended either by the fancy or the understanding. He is at once known and possessed. It is an experimental, and not a speculative knowledge that conceives him; he understands him that feels him. We see him in his grace and truth, not in any carnal or gross pretense."[31] In Ephesians

29. See Westminster Shorter Catechism, Q. 88.
30. For example, see Hoornbeeck, *Theologiae Practicae*, 1:8. The same emphases were present in Peter van Mastricht (1630–1706), among many others. See Adriaan C. Neele, *Petrus van Mastricht (1630–1706): Reformed Orthodoxy: Method and Piety* (Leiden: Brill, 2009).
31. Edward Reynolds, *Meditations on the Fall and Rising of St. Peter* (London, 1677), 58.

2:18, Paul placed the doctrine of the Trinity at the center of his doctrine of salvation. This leads to the following points of application:

1. *If we would develop a Trinitarian piety, we must first start thinking of everything that our God does in Trinitarian terms.* John Calvin once called the Trinity "God's distinctive mark."[32] The fact that God is one in essence and three in persons is what distinguishes Him from idols.[33] If we would think like Trinitarians, then let us do away with manmade illustrations of the doctrine. Some note that a man may be a father, a son, and a brother while remaining the same man, hoping to illustrate how God can be one being who is three persons. Others argue that the Trinity is like water, which can exist in solid, liquid, and gaseous forms at the same time. The problem with the first analogy is that it makes God into one being and one person. The problem with the second analogy is that it results in three beings sharing the same essence instead of retaining the unity of the persons in one undivided divine essence. The fact is that we are incapable of illustrating the triunity of God without falling into heresy.[34]

Instead, let us develop Trinitarian thinking by thinking through the works of God in terms of all three divine persons. The Father created the world through His Word, and the Spirit of God brought order to the creation (Gen. 1:1–2; John 1:3; Col. 1:16). The Father sent the Son to take a true human nature, the Holy Spirit united the divine and human natures of Christ in Mary's womb, and the God-man was born of a woman (Gal. 4:4–5). The Son offered Himself as a sacrifice to the Father by the Holy Spirit for our sins (Heb. 9:14). Christ is the image of the invisible God, and the Spirit of God restores that image in us by conforming us to Christ's image (Col. 1:15; 2 Cor. 3:18). The Father offers Christ to us in the sacraments, we feed upon Christ by faith, and He is present with us by the Holy

---

32. Cited in Douglas F. Kelly, "The True and Triune God: Calvin's Doctrine of the Holy Trinity," in David W. Hall and Peter A. Lillback, eds., *A Theological Guide to Calvin's Institutes* (Phillipsburg, N.J.: P&R Publishing, 2008), 65–89.

33. "For when the Godhead is abstracted from the Father, Son, and Holy Ghost, God is transformed into an idol.... And the unity of the Godhead is to be adored in the Trinity of persons." William Perkins (1558–1602), *An Instruction Against the Idolatry of the Last Times, And an Instruction Touching Religious or Divine Worship* (Cambridge: Iohn Legat, 1601), 5.

34. Johannes Vos, *The Westminster Larger Catechism: A Commentary* (Phillipsburg, N.J.: P&R Publishing, 2002), 26.

Spirit.[35] We pray to the Father, in the name of Christ, by the help of the Spirit. The church is the household of God (Eph. 2:19), the body of Christ (1 Cor. 12:27), and the temple of the Holy Spirit (3:16).[36] These are only a few examples of how the Trinity pervades all of the doctrines of Scripture.

The first battle of the Christian life always begins in our minds. How can we live as Trinitarians if we do not think like Trinitarians? Thomas Manton wrote, "We were made for understanding this mystery."[37]

2. *The triune nature of God sets the pattern for unity amid our diversity in the church.* We must be imitators of God as beloved children (Eph. 5:1). We imitate Christ's character, but as Manton said, "Let us study to imitate the Trinity."[38] Christ renews us in the image of God by the Spirit by enabling us to keep the commandments of God, but this is not the only way in which we become like God. The unity of the Godhead means that the church is one. Therefore, let us be one in our affections. Let us study, pray, and strive to be one in faith, to speak the same things, and to be of one mind in light of Scripture. However, the plurality of persons in the Godhead is the reason why, even though the church is one, yet its members have diverse functions. The diversity of our gifts and labors in the church reflects the glorious diversity in our God.

Are you ever discouraged because you feel that you are not as useful as another church member? Have you envied the place that God gave to them and not to you? Rest in the fact that even the differences among us better enable us to reflect the glory of God. There is no inferiority among the persons of the Trinity, yet there is diversity in operation. Count it a great honor to imitate the Trinity.

---

35. Richard Sibbes (1577–1635) applied the Trinity to the Lord's Supper in a very striking manner: "In the Sacrament see the Father." The Spirit is then the linking factor between believers and the Father and the Son: "The Spirit of the Father and the Son must discover the love of the Father to us in his Son." Richard Sibbes, *The Works of Richard Sibbes* (reprint, Edinburgh: Banner of Truth, 1976), 4:329–30.

36. Francis Turretin (1623–1687) wrote, "The church is the primary work of the holy Trinity, the object of Christ's mediation and the subject of the application of his benefits." Francis Turretin, *Institutes of Elenctic Theology*, ed. James T. Dennison Jr., trans. George Musgrave Giger (Phillipsburg, N.J.: P&R Publishing, 1997), 3:1. For more information on the Trinity in connection to the church, see Edmund P. Clowney, *The Church* (Downer's Grove, Ill.: InterVarsity Press, 1995), 13–60.

37. Manton, *Works*, 11:104.

38. Manton, *Works*, 10:333; 11:36.

3. *Ministers should labor to be Trinitarian in their preaching.* The implications of Ephesians 2:18 for the relation of the doctrine of the Trinity to ministers' personal piety is a clear example of why they should never limit their sermon preparation to Bible commentaries. There are many useful commentaries on Ephesians, but almost all of them completely gloss over the importance of Paul's Trinitarian statement in this passage. Perhaps the reason for this is that theological studies have become too compartmentalized. Seminaries split courses into systematic theology, biblical theology and exegesis, historical theology, and practical theology. There is nothing inherently wrong with this approach. However, if ministers do not draw from all of these areas to some extent, they will impoverish their preaching.[39]

Ministers, you need to understand Paul's Trinitarianism in light of the unfolding plan of God in history. You need to understand how his teaching relates to the doctrines of the Bible as a whole. You must weave this doctrine into the heart of your own devotion and Christian practice. You will do this only if you study broadly and prayerfully. Your people need a God who is triune. The triune God is the only God who saves. If you would teach your congregations to be practical Trinitarians through your teaching and preaching, then you must first teach yourselves.

4. *The work of the triune God should comfort us greatly.* We have three divine and almighty persons working for our good and our eternal salvation. These three agree perfectly in their work, and they work for our salvation. The triune God cannot fail in His purposes. Will the Father, who chose us in Christ before time began, let us slip from His grasp? Will the Son lose the fruit of His agonizing death on the cross and of the plan that He and the Father agreed upon from eternity past? Will the Spirit allow the work of the Father and of the Son to be in vain by failing to apply the work of Christ to the elect, or by allowing them to fall away from grace?

Let your faith rest upon the glorious Trinity. Rest in the one true God and in each person in particular. If the work of all three persons of the Godhead cannot comfort you, then what can? If you have

---

39. While his program for integrating theological studies may be overambitious, Richard Muller provides a thought-provoking analysis of this problem in *The Study of Theology: From Biblical Interpretation to Contemporary Formulation* (Grand Rapids: Zondervan, 1991).

weak faith, ask the Spirit to sustain what little faith you have. If you are troubled by the prevalence of the sin that remains in you, go to Christ, who has removed both the guilt and the power of sin on behalf of His people. When you feel alone and abandoned, cast off the doubts that Satan whispers into your ear. Look to your Father in heaven, who has proved His love to you by sending two divine persons to ensure that you can call Him your Father. Do you not see that every deficiency of the Christian life results from looking to ourselves rather than looking in faith to each person in the Godhead to supply what we lack?

Conclusion

My goal has been to give you the necessary building blocks to becoming self-consciously Trinitarian in your daily walk with God. May these thoughts be the start of a gloriously enriched experience of communion with God in your life. May you think and live as the apostle Paul did as you come to the Father, through Christ, by the Spirit, in every day that you live and in everything that you do.

Contributors

DR. JOEL R. BEEKE is President and Professor of Systematic Theology and Homiletics at Puritan Reformed Theological Seminary in Grand Rapids, Michigan. He also serves as a pastor of the Heritage Netherlands Reformed congregation in Grand Rapids, and as editorial director of Reformation Heritage Books. He is the author of several dozens of books and a few thousand articles published in journals, periodicals, and encyclopedias. He also speaks at numerous conferences around the world.

DR. GERALD BILKES is Professor of New Testament and Biblical Theology at Puritan Reformed Theological Seminary. He has written a book on Christ's parables and several articles on biblical-theological themes. He also serves as a pastor in the Free Reformed Churches of North America.

REV. BART ELSHOUT is a graduate of Puritan Reformed Theological Seminary. He has served as pastor in the Heritage Reformed Congregations in Jordan, Ontario and Chilliwack, B.C. He also served as an evangelist in Denver, Colorado for five years. He has translated Wilhelmus à Brakel's *The Christian's Reasonable Service* and several other works from Dutch to English. He is currently an emeritus pastor in the Heritage Netherlands Reformed Congregations and resides in Pompton Plains, New Jersey.

REV. RYAN MCGRAW is the pastor of First Orthodox Presbyterian Church, Sunnyvale, California. He is the author of *The Day of Worship: Reassessing the Christian Life in Light of the Sabbath; By Good and Necessary Consequence;* and *Christ's Glory, Your Good.*

DR. DAVID MURRAY is Professor of Old Testament and Practical Theology at Puritan Reformed Theological Seminary. He was a pastor for twelve years, first at Lochcarron Free Church of Scotland and then at Stornoway Free Church of Scotland (Continuing). From 2002–2007, he was Lecturer in Hebrew and Old Testament at the Free Church Seminary in Inverness. He has a Doctor of Ministry degree from Reformation International Theological

Seminary for his work relating Old Testament Introduction studies to the pastoral ministry.

REV. BURK PARSONS is editor of *Tabletalk* magazine and co-pastor at Saint Andrew's Chapel in Sanford, Florida. He is the author of *Why Do we Have Creeds* along with dozens of articles for *Tabletalk* magazine.

DR. DEREK W. H. THOMAS is the Minister of Teaching at First Presbyterian Church of Columbia, South Carolina, and Visiting Professor of Systematic and Practical Theology at Reformed Theological Seminary in Atlanta, Georgia. He has written or edited dozens of books, and serves as the Editorial Director for the Alliance of Confessing Evangelicals and the editor of its e-zine, Reformation 21. He also speaks at numerous conferences around the world.

DR. WILLIAM VANDOODEWAARD is Associate Professor of Church History at Puritan Reformed Theological Seminary. He previously taught at Patrick Henry College and Huntington University. Dr. VanDoodewaard is an author and writer for numerous academic journals and other periodicals. He is an ordained minister in the Associate Reformed Presbyterian Church.

REV. PAUL SMALLEY serves as a Teaching Assistant for Dr. Joel Beeke at the Puritan Reformed Theological Seminary. He formerly served as a pastor for more than ten years and graduated with his ThM degree from PRTS.